Alfred Hitchcock

On Directors Series

John Ford
Quentin Tarantino

www.booksites.net/mclean

Alfred

Hitchcock

Nicholas Haeffner

PEARSON
Longman

Harlow, England • London • New York • Boston • San Francisco • Toronto
Sydney • Tokyo • Singapore • Hong Kong • Seoul • Taipei • New Delhi
Cape Town • Madrid • Mexico City • Amsterdam • Munich • Paris • Milan

Pearson Education Limited
Edinburgh Gate
Harlow
Essex CM20 2JE
England

and Associated Companies throughout the world

Visit us on the World Wide Web at:
www.pearsoned.co.uk

First published 2005

© Pearson Education Limited 2005

ISBN 0 582 43738 5

British Library Cataloguing-in-Publication Data
A catalogue record for this book is available from the British Library

Library of Congress Cataloging-in-Publication Data
Haeffner, Nicholas.
  Alfred Hitchcock / Nicholas Haeffner.
    p. cm. — (On directors series)
  Includes bibliographical references and index.
  ISBN 0–582–43738–5
  1. Hitchcock, Alfred, 1899—Criticism and interpretation.   I. Title.   II. Series.

PN1998.3.H58H34 2004
791.4302′33′092—dc22

                                                    2004048495

10   9   8   7   6   5   4   3   2   1
09   08   07   06   05

Typeset in 10/13pt Giovanni Book by 35
Printed and bound in China
PPLC/01

The publisher's policy is to use paper manufactured from sustainable forests.

B+T - A/00

Contents

Publisher's acknowledgements

We are grateful to the following for permission to reproduce the pictures that appear in this book:

ABC Photography Archives for *Notorious*, *Rebecca* and *Spellbound*; Canal+ Image UK Ltd for *Blackmail*; London Features International for *The Lodger* reproduced courtesy of itv plc (Granada International)/LFI; Patricia H. O'Connell and Leland H. Faust, Trustees of the Alfred J. Hitchcock Trust, for images on pages 7, 33, 42 and 51; Universal Studios Licensing LLLP for *Psycho* © 1960 Shamley Productions, Inc., *Marnie* © 1964 Geoffrey Stanley, Inc. and *Vertigo* © 1958 Universal City Studios, Inc. for Samuel Taylor and Patricia Hitchcock O'Connell as trustees.

All pictures kindly provided by the British Film Institute.

In some instances we have been unable to trace the owners of copyright material, and we would appreciate any information that would enable us to do so.

Acknowledgements

Writing a book on Hitchcock proved to be a tall order. The number of films made by Hitchcock, the detail with which they were conceived and the volume of critical commentary on them, is quite formidable. Luckily, I had help. I would like to thank the following for their hard work in the preparation of this book: Julia Hallam, Alan Lovell, Paul McDonald, Ken MacKinnon and Bill Schwarz all read sections of the book and provided invaluable feedback. Alexander Ballinger, Paul Cobley and Christopher Williams devoted considerable time and effort to careful reading of the initial drafts, and a great many of their comments and suggestions have found their way into the final version. Brian Burge, Sarah Bury, Mary Lince and Gavin McLean made sure that things moved quickly and efficiently at the publishing end. Finally, my biggest thanks go to Jane Goodall, Paul Haeffner, Margaret Haeffner and especially Nicolai Hart Hansen, who provided unfailing support when the going got tough.

Films directed by Alfred Hitchcock

1926 The Pleasure Garden
1926 The Mountain Eagle
1926 The Lodger: a Story of the London Fog
1927 Downhill
1927 Easy Virtue
1927 The Ring
1928 The Farmer's Wife
1928 Champagne
1929 The Manxman
1929 Blackmail
1929 Juno and the Paycock
1930 Elstree Calling (linking sections only)
1930 Murder!
1931 The Skin Game
1931 Rich and Strange
1932 Number Seventeen
1934 Waltzes From Vienna
1934 The Man Who Knew Too Much
1935 The 39 Steps
1936 Secret Agent
1936 Sabotage
1937 Young and Innocent
1938 The Lady Vanishes
1939 Jamaica Inn
1940 Rebecca
1940 Foreign Correspondent
1941 Mr and Mrs Smith
1941 Suspicion
1942 Saboteur
1943 Shadow of a Doubt
1944 Lifeboat
1944 Bon Voyage (short)
1944 Aventure Malgache (short)
1945 Spellbound
1946 Notorious

1948	The Paradine Case
1948	Rope
1949	Under Capricorn
1950	Stage Fright
1950	Strangers on a Train
1951	I Confess
1954	Dial M for Murder
1954	Rear Window
1954	To Catch a Thief
1955	The Trouble with Harry
1956	The Man Who Knew Too Much
1957	The Wrong Man
1957	Vertigo
1959	North by Northwest
1960	Psycho
1963	The Birds
1964	Marnie
1966	Torn Curtain
1969	Topaz
1972	Frenzy
1976	Family Plot

There are different conventions regarding these dates. I have chosen to use Charles Barr's *English Hitchcock* and Jane Sloan's *Alfred Hitchcock: The Definitive Filmography* to provide these dates.

Background

Alfred Hitchcock was a genius: at least, according to his biographer Donald Spoto, author of *The Dark Side of Genius: The Life of Alfred Hitchcock* (1983). But what exactly does the word 'genius' mean when we apply it to Hitchcock? Is it possible that it conceals more than it reveals? Before the nineteenth century, the word 'genius' more commonly referred to the origins and nature of a whole culture. It later came to mean a kind of unique spirit animating an individual. Perhaps it is the case that Hitchcock possessed an exceptional spirit – a will to create, to invent, to represent the world anew. But in Spoto's famous biography, something more is added to this perspective on the director, which is the idea of a tormented and woman-hating spirit animating the man and his work. Spoto's book has been extremely successful, not least in helping to define how the public perceives the director and his films. This study, however, takes issue with Spoto's interpretation and, to a lesser extent, with the work of critics who have used psychoanalysis to investigate the man and his films.

This book is less interested in the concept of the Freudian unconscious or in the torment said to lurk deep inside Hitchcock. Instead, the force which has been called Hitchcock's genius will be seen to originate not in his psyche or personality, but in his objective social and economic situation. As such, his films are seen to emerge out of class relations, cultural traditions, economic necessities, industrial imperatives, friendships, alliances and enmities. Instead of trying to look inside the soul of the artist in order to explain his films, it is better to begin by looking outside at the contexts of class, culture and commerce in which his film-making was embedded. His films are seen to germinate not in some inner essence but in relationships. Hitchcock's films are also preoccupied with relationships, most especially those between people and the everyday objects of their perception. The word *'object'* here should be understood as referring to things (like the glass of milk in *Suspicion* (1941) which appears to glow when the heroine of the film believes it to be poisoned) as well as human beings. Human beings

This ordinary bread knife from *Blackmail* (1929), becomes an object of terror for the heroine, Alice White (Anny Ondra). Courtesy of Canal+ Image UK Ltd.

can be treated like things when they become the object of desires and fears, as in the duplicitous Judy/Madeleine (Kim Novak) in *Vertigo* (1957) who is turned into a screen for the projected fantasies of Scottie (James Stewart).

There is also a connection between Hitchcock's fascination with relationships and the thriller form in which he usually worked. The thriller writer John Le Carré once explained in a radio interview that his books were only partly about international espionage. The appeal of the spy thriller, he claimed, lay in its ability to dramatise the problem of trust in everyday relationships, such as work and marriage. It is perhaps no surprise that Hitchcock should find that his interest in relationships was ideally expressed through the thriller genre, earning him the title 'master of suspense'.

Alfred Joseph Hitchcock was born in 1899 in Leytonstone, a suburb of East London, to William and Emma Hitchcock, a lower-middle-class Catholic couple, who owned and ran a grocery and poultry shop. He was the youngest of three children and was brought up a strict Catholic. He repeatedly told a story of how, as a child, his father had played a cruel trick on him, arranging for the boy to be locked up in a local police cell to teach him a lesson. Hitchcock would often trot out this story as a pat psychological explanation of his later filmic obsessions. Indeed, it is not certain that the story is even true. However, there are memorable images of the police and other figures associated with the law in many of his films. The menacing traffic cop in *Psycho* (1960), shot in close-up with his eyes hidden behind dark glasses is perhaps the best-known example.

At the age of 11 he was sent to St Ignatius, a Jesuit school in Stamford Hill, London. He was by his own account a lonely child with a penchant for practical jokes, a hobby which remained with him for the rest of his life. Hitchcock buried himself in magazines, novels, films and plays, developing an enthusiasm for the macabre stories of Edgar Allan Poe. Mogg (1999) describes the impression made on Hitchcock by Oscar Wilde's *The Picture of Dorian Gray*, Flaubert's *Madame Bovary* and Charles Dickens' *Bleak House*, especially the latter with its dark atmosphere and memorable characters.

Hitchcock's father died in 1914, creating a financial crisis and strengthening the already close bond between the boy and his mother. However, instead of going into his father's business on leaving school, he began working for the Henley Telegraph Company in 1915, first as a clerk and then in the advertising department where he could exercise his talent for drawing. During this time he attended evening classes run by the University of London, where he pursued an interest in art. Later in life, Hitchcock built up a small collection of modern art, including works by Paul Klee and Maurice Vlaminck.

In 1920, keen to break into the film industry, Hitchcock secured a menial job designing titles at Famous Players-Lasky, an American-owned studio in North London. In a short time he was head of the titles department, which devised and supervised the text that was inserted into the silent films produced by the company. These intertitles provided lines of dialogue and the pieces of information which the audience required to follow the story. At this time, the job of devising the titles involved an element of scriptwriting, so Hitchcock had some creative input into the stories.

In 1922 Famous Players-Lasky pulled out of their Islington studios and began renting the property to Michael Balcon and Victor Saville, who formed Gainsborough Pictures. At this time, Hitchcock was working as an assistant to director Graham Cutts. He was also given credit for scenario and set design on *Woman to Woman* (1922), *The Passionate Adventure* (1924), *The Blackguard* (1925), and *The Prude's Fall* (1925). Balcon recognised Hitchcock's skills and, against the urging of Cutts, offered to let him try his hand at directing. It was under his patronage that Hitchcock first displayed his precocious talents. Hitchcock was later to pay tribute to Balcon's influence, saying: 'I have been allowed to experiment. This I owe to one man, Michael Balcon. Balcon, Director of Productions at the Gaumont British studios, has been associated with me since I began. It is he who has allowed me to follow my celluloid whims' (Gottlieb, 1997, p. 249). Balcon also introduced Hitchcock to Alma Reville, a film editor and scriptwriter, to whom Hitchcock proposed in 1923. They were eventually married in 1926. Reville was highly thought of within the industry, particularly for her editing skills, and there was even some talk of her being given a film to direct. However, she sidelined her personal career and remained Hitchcock's closest advisor and working associate throughout his career. In 1928 Alma gave birth to their only child, Patricia, who later appeared in *Stage Fright* (1950), *Strangers on a Train* (1950) and *Psycho*.

The director carefully cultivated his public persona, forming a company, Hitchcock Baker Productions, in 1930, for the sole purpose of 'advertising to the press the newsworthiness' of himself (Spoto, 1983, p. 138). However, by this point in his career, his struggle to combine both commercial and artistic success had already resulted in damaging attacks on him, first from the chief distributor, C.M. Woolf, who in 1926 tried to block the release of four Hitchcock films, and then from influential critics such as John Grierson. But Hitchcock was becoming a well-known name and by the time of his fourth film, *Downhill* (1927), *The Bioscope* could already claim that 'the selling angle is the name of Hitchcock' (Spoto, 1983, p. 98).

Hitchcock joined British International Pictures (BIP) under the direction of producer John Maxwell in 1927 for a record fee, making him the highest paid director in the country at only 28 years old. *The Bioscope* lauded *The Ring* (1927) as 'the most magnificent picture ever made' but the more highbrow journal *Close Up* dismissed it as overpraised. However, a review in *The London Evening News* understood the direction that Hitchcock's work was taking when it wrote that *The Ring* 'succeeds in that very rare accomplishment of being the purest art film and a fine popular entertainment' (Ryall, 1996, p. 93). During his stint at BIP, Hitchcock struggled to make various genres of film, including comedy, romantic melodrama and even a musical to which he discovered he was unsuited. However, during this period he began to explore the possibilities of manipulating space (through creative camera placement), time (through editing) and psychology (through the insertion of subjective shots). This experimentation can be seen in *The Farmer's Wife* (1928), where the camera cuts backwards and forwards between the widowed farmer, lost in contemplation, and a succession of shots of imagined possible wives in his actually empty fireside chair. Shots of the empty chair alternating with shots of the farmer looking at the chair, lost in thought, are used at various times in the film to suggest the past (loss), the fear of the future (loneliness), hope (imagined companionship) and fear (committing himself to an unsuitable partner). This pattern forms a repeated motif in the film and offers the spectator an objective representation of the farmer's subjective thoughts and feelings. Through Hitchcock's manipulation of editing and camera work, we share, as Paul Jensen puts it, 'not just a point of view, but a subjective mental state'

(2000, p. 37). The opening of *Champagne* (1928) has an audacious trick shot of a ballroom apparently seen through the bottom of a glass, while *The Manxman* (1929) features a dissolve from the dark, bubbling surface of the sea where a despairing woman has attempted suicide to an inkwell in a courtroom into which her lover, a judge, dips his pen nib. This dialectical movement between subjective experience and brute objectivity developed early in the films and became a cornerstone of Hitchcock's cinematic technique.

Although Hitchcock's visual language was beginning to develop, it wasn't until he signed a deal with Balcon's Gaumont British Pictures in 1934 that he found his niche with a series of suspense thrillers made in partnership with the writer Charles Bennett. The 'thriller sextet' as it has become known comprises *The Man Who Knew Too Much* (1934), *The 39 Steps* (1935), *Secret Agent* (1936), *Sabotage* (1936), *Young and Innocent* (1937) and *The Lady Vanishes* (1938) (the latter scripted by Frank Launder and Sydney Gilliat). It was during this period that Hitchcock (with considerable help from Bennett and Alma Hitchcock) established his public reputation and many of the technical, aesthetic and entrepreneurial strategies that would be perfected in his later American films.

During this period, he wrote a great many articles for various publications outlining his thoughts and opinions on the domestic film industry, going out of his way frequently to praise the American approach to cinema as technically superior to that of the British. He complained that 'one of the chief disadvantages of British film production is the scarcity of people with an instinct for films – who can, in fact, think pictorially' (Gottlieb, 1997, p. 174). However, his criticisms of English cinema were social as well as technical. First, there was his championship of the German and Soviet cinema, which he felt was unappreciated in the insular culture of England. Then there was his admiration for the socially-inclusive American film, which he compared favourably to the socially restricted British one. Finally, there was his campaign to reform the British cinema by arguing the need for more and better representations of what he called the ordinary middle classes on the screen.

From the start, Hitchcock's cosmopolitan tastes in cinema stopped short of admiration for his own country's productions. The directors he praised were the American D.W. Griffith and the Germans Fritz Lang and F.W. Murnau. Although he tended to shy away from naming individual films, producers or directors, he nevertheless took the opportunity to criticise what he called in a 1934 article for the journal *Film Weekly* 'Stodgy British Pictures'. He praised the American cinema for its use of 'imaginative backgrounds': 'They give us pictures about telephone exchanges, icemen, newspaper reporters, police cars, repair gangs – anything and everything under the sun. They make the most of every possible setting for their stories.' He went on to criticise 'our drawing room school of drama' for its lack of freshness (Gottlieb, 1997, p. 170). The problem, as he saw it, was not with British film production as a whole, but rather with 'a hard enemy, the film of chromium plating, dress shirts, cocktails, and Oxford accents which is being continually made with the idea that it shows English life' (ibid., p. 178).

In 'More Cabbages, Fewer Kings: A Believer in the Little Man', an article published in a 1937 edition of *Kinematograph Weekly*, he wrote that 'British film producers know only two strata of English existence, the poor and the rich' (ibid., p. 176). He argued that a 'vital central stratum of British humanity, the middle class' had been ignored in British films (ibid., p. 177). 'The higher you run up the British social scale', Hitchcock argued, 'the faster the drama dies. The veneer of civilisation is so thick among the rich that individual qualities are killed. . . . Voices are the same, expressions are nil, personalities are suppressed. The upper classes are too "bottled up" to be of any use as colourful screen matter, too stiffened with breeding to relax into the natural easiness and normality required by the screen' (ibid., p. 177). However, the upper classes do feature as central characters in several of Hitchcock's early films, like *The Skin Game* (1931), and they are portrayed with some positive characteristics. Sir John (Herbert Marshall) in *Murder!* (1930), for example, is an upper-class character who is noble and just. Most of these representations, however, tell us less about Hitchcock's attitude towards class and more about the conventions of middlebrow drama and literature of the period.

Hitchcock could be an astute observer of English cultural identity in his writings, such as when he spoke of the characteristics of English drama with its 'implications of long-suppressed passions, released in devious and tortuous ways' (Gottlieb, 1997, p. 135). His films also consciously refer to Englishness and Britishness, both verbally and visually. For instance, in *Blackmail* (1929), scripted by Charles Bennett, one of the characters complains: 'A good clean whack over the 'ead is one thing – there's something British about that. But knives, no, knives is not right.' While American films were superior technically ('slick, smart, efficient to the nth degree'), Hitchcock argued that, 'to British audiences they are frequently lacking in what, for want of a better word, we call "soul"' (ibid., p. 173). But this remark could have been made with a self-serving intention as he goes on to defend 'the product of individuality, in which one guiding mind is behind the whole production' (ibid., p. 173). Hitchcock was to become famous for this sort of personality-led film-making.

The Lady Vanishes, apparently a quintessential Hitchcock film, with its blend of suspense, humour and romance, was a project taken over at an

Alfred, Alma and Patricia Hitchcock bound for the US in 1939. Courtesy of Patricia H. O'Connell and Leland H. Faust, Trustees of the Alfred J. Hitchcock Trust.

advanced stage from another director, Roy William Neil. However, Hitchcock's direction of the Launder and Gilliat script gained considerable attention for him in America where *Variety* wrote that the film 'minus the deft and artistic handling of the director, despite its cast and photography, would not stand up for Grade A candidacy'. *Kine Weekly* was of the opinion that 'the direction of this film amounts to genius inasmuch as a wildly improbable plot is converted into gripping entertainment' (Ryall, 1996, p. 110).

Aware that British films lacked what he called the 'glitter or glamour' necessary for great box-office success, Hitchcock looked around for a deal with an American company. But like his friend and fellow *émigré* Cary Grant, Hitchcock was not only attracted by the money and glamour of the American film industry when he went to work there for producer David O. Selznick in 1939. He was also repelled by the English class system and felt stifled by the mores of English society (McCann, 1996). Selznick's idea of cinema was very different from Balcon's. Where Balcon sought realism and later a commitment to 'projecting Britain and the British character' (Barr, 1993, p. 7), Selznick's name was synonymous with the grand Hollywood studio style of films such as *Gone With the Wind* (1939). But Hitchcock sometimes found Selznick's ideas crass and corny. For *Rebecca* (1940), Hitchcock remembers, 'He wanted the house to go up in flames, and for the smoke to form the letter "R". Imagine!' (Bogdanovich, 1997, p. 508). However, Selznick's detailed criticisms of Hitchcock's shooting scripts left a lasting impression on the director, encouraging him to concentrate his camera on people rather than things. On *Rebecca*, Selznick got Hitchcock to leaven his 'montage-driven' approach with longer takes and slicker, more conventional editing patterns which reinforced the emotions of the characters rather than showcasing cinematic technique. Selznick, who by this time had become associated with women's films, also encouraged Hitchcock to pay attention to 'the little feminine things which are so recognisable and which make every woman say [of the heroine], "I know just how she feels . . . I know just what she's going through". . . etc' (Leff, 1987, p. 45).

Selznick had Hitchcock under contract for eight years but only produced three of his films, *Rebecca, Spellbound* (1945) and *The Paradine Case* (1948). The rest of the time Selznick hired Hitchcock out to other studios for a substantial fee, which he pocketed. There is some speculation that Hitchcock had Lars Thorwald, the seedy wife murderer in *Rear Window* (1954), made up to look like Selznick as a form of revenge for the latter's 'tyranny' during the time that Hitchcock was under contract to him. *Rebecca*, based on the gothic romance by Daphne du Maurier, established Hitchcock as a star director in America, although he felt that the film belonged more to Selznick, who won an Oscar for it, and was frustrated at what he felt were the creative compromises that he had been forced into. The film was a spectacular calling card to Hollywood from the director, showing a mastery of the grand studio style which Hitchcock had so envied while working in England. Characteristically, Hitchcock was critical of the leads (Laurence Olivier and Joan Fontaine) he had been assigned, although he worked successfully again with Fontaine on *Suspicion*. As with the later *Strangers on a Train*, Hitchcock seemed far more interested in the character of the psychopath, here Mrs Danvers (Judith Anderson), than in the romantic couple at the supposed centre of the film.

Back in England, the death of Hitchcock's mother in 1942 was followed closely by the apparent suicide of his brother William. Hitchcock found consolation in food. By 1943, at 300 pounds, the director was dangerously overweight, which led him to embark on a well-publicised diet, during the course of which he lost nearly 100 pounds. Hitchcock marked the conclusion of the diet by making his trademark personal appearance in *Lifeboat* (1944) as the before and after photo in a newpaper 'lose weight' advertisement.

During the Second World War, he made some contribution to the anti-fascist cause with films such as *Foreign Correspondent* (1940) and *Saboteur* (1942), although *Lifeboat*, whose message was intended to be one of allied solidarity against fascism, was criticised for seeming to be too sympathetic to a Nazi character. Back in England, his former friend and ally Michael Balcon publicly attacked Hitchcock for deserting his country and not contributing to the war effort. On 25 August 1940, Balcon denounced Hitchcock in the *Sunday Dispatch* newspaper for working in America at a time when his country required a demonstration of his loyalty and called him a 'deserter'. Balcon wrote,

> *I had a plump young junior technician in my studios whom I promoted from department to department. Today he is one of our most famous directors and he is in Hollywood while we are left behind short-handed and trying to harness the films to our great national effort.*
>
> *(Spoto, 1983, p. 235)*

Hitchcock was much aggrieved by this attack and replied that he could only imagine that Balcon's remarks had been motivated by 'personal jealousy'. The director argued that he was helping his country in his own way by promoting British talent abroad. He even returned to England to direct two wartime propaganda shorts, *Bon Voyage* (1944) and *Aventure Malgache* (1944), as a more direct contribution to the war effort at home. In 1945 he was hired as 'treatment advisor' on a documentary about the Nazi Holocaust entitled *Memory of the Camps*, which was made for the Supreme Headquarters of the Allied Expeditionary Force but was never released. A copy of it is held at the Imperial War Museum.

Hitchcock grew frustrated and resentful in his collaboration with Selznick, eventually striking out in partnership with the English business-man Sidney Bernstein, a friend from the British Film Society in the 1920s, to form Transatlantic Pictures. Bernstein was a highly successful business-man who founded the Granada chain of cinemas in 1930 and went on to found Granada TV. He was also an intellectual with left-wing sympathies who was interested in filmic experimentation. Together they co-produced *Rope* (1948) and *Under Capricorn* (1949). However, Hitchcock's newly acquired obsession with filming in long, uninterrupted takes to give the illusion that no editing was taking place, contributed to the perceived stiffness of both the films, which had been troubled productions. The commercial failure of these two films led to the collapse of Transatlantic Pictures and to the termination of the partnership between Hitchcock and Bernstein. From here on Hitchcock returned to making films for the major studios, now, however, as producer of his own films.

Hitchcock's relationship with Lew Wasserman, chairman of MCA Pictures, was more durable and profitable. Wasserman was a formidable businessman who became Hitchcock's agent in 1946. It was at his urging that Hitchcock launched the television series, *Alfred Hitchcock Presents*, in 1955. The series made Hitchcock immensely rich and famous throughout the world, with spin-offs including records (such as *Music to be Murdered By*), board games, and short-story anthologies, making Hitchcock's name and bulbous profile instantly recognisable by the public.

Hitchcock signed a deal with Paramount Pictures, for whom he produced a string of his most highly regarded films: *Rear Window, To Catch a Thief* (1955), *The Trouble With Harry* (1955), *The Man Who Knew Too Much* (1956) and *Vertigo*. Much of the credit for these films must also go to the quality of the talent he was now able to attract. For the first time in his career, he assembled a regular team which included costume designer Edith Head, cameraman Robert Burks, set designer Henry Bumstead, editor George Tomasini and, most important of all, composer Bernard Herrmann. His films also established a reputation for glamorous stars (Grace Kelly, Cary Grant, Kim Novak) and striking use of locations (Marrakesh, the French Riviera, San Francisco, Vermont).

North by Northwest (1959), written for Hitchcock by Ernest Lehman with the intention of producing the 'ultimate Hitchcock film', encapsulated much of what the public had come to associate with the Hitchcock trade-mark. One reviewer, A.H. Weiler in the *New York Times*, noticed Hitchcock's strategy of turning a tourist's gaze on American culture when he described the film as 'a suspenseful and delightful Cook's Tour of some of the more photogenic spots in the United States'.

Psycho was an unexpected hit with a younger generation of Hitchcock fans who had come to know of him through his television show. However, this film, and even more so its successor, *The Birds* (1963), alienated many of his older audience by pushing the envelope of taste and experimentation beyond their limits. By the 1960s Hitchcock's career was, along with the rest of the older generation in Hollywood, on a relative downturn with *Marnie* (1964), *Torn Curtain* (1966) and *Topaz* (1969) all performing poorly at the box office. However, his critical reputation began to soar, particularly as a result of a set of interviews with the French film-maker and critic, François Truffaut, which was published in book form in 1965. Truffaut and Claude Chabrol of the French film journal *Cahiers du Cinéma* had first met Hitchcock in 1955 and there is no doubt that the association had an effect on Hitchcock's attitude to his film-making, especially with *The Birds*, which saw Hitchcock under the influence of European art cinema.

Constantly overweight and with a tendency to eat and drink too much, Hitchcock's health began to fail seriously in the 1970s. After returning to England to make *Frenzy* in 1972, which was widely hailed as a return to form, he completed only one more film, *Family Plot* (1976), a romantic crime caper, before ill health forced him to retire during the planning of *The Short Night*, which remained un-filmed. He died of heart, liver and kidney disorders on 29 April 1980.

In trying to assess this legacy, it is very tempting to posit such links between circumstances of Hitchcock's life, his personality and his work. For instance, Peter Bogdanovich, who knew the director well, saw the origins of Hitchcock's drive to make films in Hitchcock's body itself. 'Life typecasts us', Hitchcock once told an interviewer. 'Look at me. Do you think I would have chosen to look like this? I would have preferred to play a leading man in life. I would have been Cary Grant' (in McCann, 1996, p. 211). At one point in his career Hitchcock weighed 300 pounds. Teased, bullied and isolated as a child, Bogdanovich believes that Hitchcock's films were a revenge on the world for the trick life had played on him by making him overweight and unattractive to women. In another account, given by John Houseman, who worked on *Saboteur*, the director was 'a man of exaggeratedly delicate sensibilities, marked by a harsh Catholic education and the scars from a social system against which he was in perpetual revolt' (in Krohn, 2000, p. 40). However, this kind of psychologising tends to be reductive – Hitchcock's physical apprearance and his Catholic upbringing may have been factors which motivated him but neither give us the key to understanding his work.

Hitchcock's chief conscious concerns can be seen as practical, and a good deal of his motivation was profit-driven. It makes sense to insist on the centrality of Hitchcock the businessman, working in a culture industry, in any consideration of his films partly because this image was so close to his own self-understanding. In an interview with Patrick McGilligan, he discussed the relationship between cinema and art saying

We all know that cinema is an art form of the twentieth century, but it carries with it many liabilities. What would a painter think if I handed him a canvas and said that it cost $750,000; here's an easel which costs $500,000; here's a box of paints which costs $250,000; here's a palette which costs $800,000 and a set of brushes that costs $500,000? Now paint me a picture and at least get me my money back.

(McGilligan, 1997, pp. 261–2)

He also claimed that 'one of the great misfortunes was when someone had the bright idea of calling the place that films were made a "studio" with all its artistic overtones, rather than a factory' (Taylor, 1978, p. 41).

Although he sometimes compared himself to a painter or a musician (see Gottlieb, 1997; Samuels, 1972), he dressed like a businessman and socialised with businessmen. Joseph Stefano, writer of the screenplay for *Psycho*, recalls how the creative process would always come a poor second to Hitchcock's interest in money: 'One of the easiest times for anyone to get in to see Hitchcock was whenever he was in conference with a writer. Lew Wasserman [Hitchcock's agent] used to come in and they'd talk stocks and money, money, money' (in Rebello, 1990, p. 41). Hitchcock himself commented, 'I have few friends, businessmen mostly' (ibid., p. 177). Among these friends were notable entrepreneurs such as Wasserman, Michael Balcon and Sidney Bernstein. In order to make his films, Hitchcock had to convince his investors that they stood a good chance of recouping a considerable investment at the box office and, inevitably, this affected the way in which he conceived his films. Yet Hitchcock's black humour revealed a cynicism about financial institutions and he retained a rebellious attitude towards the studio system until the end of his career, when he had become a pillar of the Hollywood establishment. The following anecdote comes from the filming of *Family Plot*, his last completed picture:

Knowing that Hitchcock owned a sizeable amount of MCA stock, Bruce Dern, one of the stars, suggested they paint the garage door in the film with graffiti of the Jaws *logo, an MCA financed hit. Hitchcock replied, 'No Bruce, I know what we should write – Fuck MCA!'*

(Sloan, 1995, p. 11)

To insist on the importance of Hitchcock as chiefly a practically-minded film-maker and businessman is not to invalidate the higher-minded claims made for his films. But it does indicate that the elements of aesthetic experimentation, moral enquiry and social criticism which have been identified in the films need to be situated within the industrial imperatives and constraints which govern the film industry. These elements also need to be placed within some kind of cultural context if we are to understand the relationship between what the poet T.S. Eliot called 'tradition and the individual talent'.

In the following chapter, Hitchcock's early influences will be considered. Far from being an interesting footnote to his work, Hitchcock's exposure to German and Russian art cinema during his years working in the British film industry, combined with his love of popular melodrama, provided him with an exemplary foundation for his career as a successful industry professional in Hollywood. More than that, his Jesuit schooling and his association with a group of intellectuals who called themselves the Film Society gave him a reflective, analytical approach. Whether in the domain of film aesthetics, basic narrative construction or business practice, Hitchcock showed the ability to break the process down into component parts and theorise it. But far from being dry and academic, this emphasis on analytical construction also embodied a playfulness and innovation, as well as a strong collaborative dimension.

1 Hitchcock's heritage: class, culture and cosmopolitanism

In an article for a French journal published in 1960, Hitchcock confessed that 'subconsciously we are always influenced by the book that we've read. The novels, the paintings, the music and all the works of art in general, form our intellectual culture from which we can't get away. Even if we want to' (Gottlieb, 1997, p. 142). Hitchcock immersed himself deeply in many different forms of culture, soaking up all he could, frequently displaying the breadth of his knowledge in interviews. Jay Presson Allen, who wrote the screenplay for *Marnie* (1964), puts Hitchcock's thirst for knowledge down to his 'sense of being uneducated. He was very defensive about class. . . . He had no education but read a lot. People like that are sponges and learn a lot from educated conversations' (in McGilligan, 1997, p. 24). It's important to establish at the outset that one of the unique features of Hitchcock's films, which partly helps to explain their status as both 'popular culture' and 'high art', lies in Hitchcock's own objective class position, which was poised between his family's working-class roots and his own cultural aspirations. The former gave him a firm grounding in popular culture, while the latter led him to absorb influences which are more usually associated with elite culture. The resulting cinema, as Hitchcock understood, was neither 'highbrow' nor 'lowbrow' but rather part of an emerging culture of the 'middlebrow'.

Hitchcock was one of the key figures in the development of a British middlebrow cinema, which aimed to combine cultural respectability with more popular sensationalist fare. Lawrence Napper has suggested that the growth of a middlebrow theatre and cinema during this time was an inevitable consequence of the emergence of the new suburban middle class 'anxious to consolidate hard-won but precarious improvement in social position and living standards' (2000, p. 115). Hitchcock frequently spoke of the need for a middle-class cinema in Britain and emphasised the distinctive qualities of English films when compared to American ones. 'My policy', he announced to the *Daily Herald*, 'is to make popular pictures which anybody can understand. But without being highbrow, I believe in making them in such a way that they will appeal to the most intelligent people as well' (Spoto, 1983, p. 135).

Although Hitchcock sought to make middlebrow films in the main-stream film industry, he was, like many other pioneer figures in cinema, something of a cultural outsider. As English Catholics, the Hitchcock family were part of a small, and to some extent dissenting, community within the wider culture of the time. The tradition of Roman Catholicism stresses the ideas of original sin and guilt. Catholicism is most obviously highlighted in the characters of Michael Logan (Montgomery Clift) in *I Confess* (1951) and Manny Balestrero (Henry Fonda) in *The Wrong Man* (1957), who are both devoutly religious. Both men take on the burden of guilt of another man, an idea which was a key motif of Hitchcock's work. But the Catholic abhorrence of sin is even more deeply woven into the texture of Hitchcock's films through the manner in which his heroes are punished for their sinful wishes as well as for their deeds. Thus the 'innocent' Guy Haines (Farley Grainger) in *Strangers on a Train* (1950) is aligned to the murderer Bruno Anthony (Robert Walker) not by action but by thought: although he did not strangle his wife, Miriam (Laura Elliot), he has already confessed in a rage that he could 'break her foul, useless little neck'.

Much Catholic culture has treated sexuality as dangerous, especially female sexuality. Since it was Eve who tempted Adam into transgression, many Catholics regard female sexuality with particular suspicion and emphasise the icons of the Madonna or Virgin (idealised) versus the whore (abject). The extent to which Catholic attitudes towards female sexuality might have influenced Hitchcock is not clear, although it might help to account for some of the representations which have been found so problematic. The images of women in one early film, *Downhill* (1927) could be seen as particularly misogynist, as Charles Barr puts it, 'all the women in this film are predatory exploiters or else ciphers' (1999, p. 46). Yet, such images are rarely so straightforwardly unsympathetic in other films such as *Notorious* (1946), which complicate stereotypical representa-tions of women through the creation of complex characters.

Hitchcock claims that the Jesuit priests at his school taught him to be disciplined and analytical, a good description of his later working method. However, the Roman Catholic Church is characterised by a love of theatricality and ritual, qualities reflected in a major thematic strand in the films. Performance and theatre are constant features of Hitchcock's films from the opening shots of his first film, *The Pleasure Garden* (1926), presenting the audience with the spectacle of dancing girls on a stage, through to classic scenes such as Mr Memory (Wylie Watson) on stage at a London music hall (*The 39 Steps*, 1935) and an assassination attempt at the

Albert Hall (*The Man Who Knew Too Much*, 1934 and 1956*).* The death of resistance fighter Juanita de Cordoba (Karin Dor) in *Topaz* (1969) is like grand opera as the camera, cutting to a very high overhead shot, shows her falling to the ground as her beautiful purple dress spreads out over the black and white tiled marble floor with extraordinary grace. The shot suggests the nobility of her struggle against political oppression, the floor resembling a chessboard where her torturer husband's political strategies are worked out with cold logic, and the dress, spreading across the floor like a pool of blood, signifying the nobility of the freedom fighters who are willing to die for their cause. Furthermore, the 'play acting' of characters such as Sir John (Herbert Marshall) in *Murder!* (1930), Alicia Huberman (Ingrid Bergman) in *Notorious*, Eve Gill (Jane Wyman) in *Stage Fright* (1950), Judy Barton (Kim Novak) in *Vertigo* (1957), Norman Bates (Anthony Perkins) in *Psycho* (1960) and Blanche Tyler (Barbara Harris) in *Family Plot* (1976) raise interesting questions about identity and demonstrate the extent to which performance in Hitchcock's films can be both playful and disturbing.

Even before his obsession with cinema had taken hold, Hitchcock had been captivated by the London theatre, which in his youth catered for a wide range of social classes. He was strongly influenced by the middlebrow tradition of the well-made play, which stretched back to nineteenth-century French comic playwrights such as Sardou, Labiche and Feydeau (Barr, 1999). This form of theatre found root in England with many playwrights (including Shaw and Rattigan), learning from its formula of well-crafted suspense, detailed plotting, fateful occurrences and mistaken identity. However, Hitchcock's stock in trade was to become his own application of devices from the well-made play, including a series of perils and pitfalls, complications and crises for the character which end each act in a cliff hanger, to the crime and suspense story, with murder becoming another key motif in his films. Already a connoisseur of the crime story (he was a regular spectator at the Old Bailey during murder trials), Hitchcock was quick to see the business opportunities in selling the English variant abroad: 'English crimes – and I am thinking particularly of murder – tend to be intrinsically more dramatic. When they do occur, perhaps because of their relative rarity, more is made of them – more juice is squeezed out, as it were; that juice is one of England's invisible exports to the United States' (Gottlieb, 1997, p. 134). The saleable subject matter of his first project, *The Lodger* (1926), with its story of a serial killer on the loose in fog-drenched London, is ironically highlighted in *Frenzy* (1972) when one of the characters, a lawyer, points out that gruesome murders are good for the tourist trade and that 'foreigners expect to see London squares fog wreathed and littered with ripped whores'. Leytonstone, where Hitchcock grew up, is no more than a few miles from Whitechapel, where the original Jack the Ripper murders were committed and it has been argued that the actual crimes and their representation in the media helped to forge dominant themes in Hitchcock's work, specifically murder, class and sexuality (the Ripper was believed to have been an upper-class gentleman preying on the underworld of Victorian prostitution) (Allen, 2000; Price, 1992).

Hitchcock's treatment of crime frequently drew on elements of theatrical melodrama. The theatre historian Michael Booth (1964), in a discussion of melodramatic conventions notes the importance of violent death. He then lists some of the dramatic forms which death can take. Examples of all of them are to be found in Hitchcock's films: stabbing (*Blackmail*, 1929), shooting (*The Man Who Knew Too Much*), hanging (*Murder!*), strangling (*Frenzy*), poisoning (*Notorious*), suicide (*Murder!*), fire (*Rebecca*, 1940), shipwreck (*Lifeboat*, 1944) and train wreck (*Secret Agent*, 1936) (Booth, 1964, p. 9). To this list might be added explosion (*Sabotage*, 1936), stabbing, beating and gassing (*Torn Curtain*, 1966) and pecking (*The Birds*, 1963). Hitchcock himself remarked that if he were to have made a film of *Cinderella*, people would want to know where the corpse was (Gottlieb, 1997, p. 145).

Hitchcock made no attempt to disguise his love of melodrama, the least socially reputable but most popular forms of theatre and film in the early part of the twentieth century. 'Melodrama', he wrote in 1936, 'came to be applied by sophisticates to the more naïve type of play or story, in which every situation was overdrawn and every emotion underlined' (1936, p. 1). He thought of it as the original source material for the cinema 'on account of its obvious physical action and physical situation' (in Gottlieb, 1997, p. 269). Melodrama began in the nineteenth century as a theatrical form which was raw, exciting and spectacular, ranging from wildly romantic to sordidly domestic. It was also shamelessly crowd-pleasing and manipulative. From it, the early cinema drew themes such as the heroine in mortal peril and the use of dramatic music to underline the action and suspense. Hitchcock could hardly have failed to be aware of its pulling power on the stages of the day. He called melodrama, with its love of sensation, 'the backbone and lifeblood of the cinema' (1936, p. 1).

The heightening of emotion through exaggerated acting gestures or body language in the early silent films (which he referred to as 'pantomiming') was a convention of silent cinema which had originated in the melodramatic theatre. 'In the early days', Hitchcock explained, 'everything depended on pantomime . . . they would make a star look agonized by telling her bad news or releasing some rats at her feet' (in Gottlieb, 1997, p. 15). In *Blackmail*, Hitchcock explains that he lit the villain in a deliberately melodramatic way, to evoke the stereotypical silent movie baddie: 'On the silent screen', he tells Truffaut, 'the villain was generally a man with a moustache. Well, my villain was clean shaven, but an ironwork chandelier in his studio cast a shadow on his upper lip, suggesting an absolutely fierce looking moustache' (in Truffaut, 1965/1986, p. 80).

Melodrama also highlighted questions of morality and often thematised men's cruelty to women. Authors such as Dickens (in novels like *Bleak House*) and Wilkie Collins (often credited with originating the suspense novel), along with women writers in the female gothic genre such as Charlotte Brontë and later Daphne du Maurier dramatised the plight of women at the hands of tyrannous men. The figure of a woman subjected to male cruelty is at the centre in many of Hitchcock's greatest films, including *Blackmail, Rebecca, Suspicion* (1941), *Notorious, Under Capricorn* (1949), *Vertigo* and *Marnie*. Although the treatment of the woman character may be strikingly sympathetic, this aspect of Hitchcock's films has not been received without ambivalence on the part of many feminists, an issue which will be explored in Chapter 5.

Villains in melodramatic narratives tended to be male and drawn from the privileged classes. *The Manxman* (1929), *Jamaica Inn* (1939), *The 39 Steps* and *The Paradine Case* (1948) all feature corrupt, callous or duplicitous justices of the peace who cloak their moral turpitude beneath a façade of class respectability and humanitarian concern. However, it is part of Hitchcock's achievement that he was also able to introduce a good deal of complexity into his best villains. Alex Sebastian (Claude Rains) in *Notorious*, although a Nazi involved in a dark plot, is also a sensitive man whose fate has a tragic aspect to it. Bruno Anthony (Robert Walker) in *Strangers on a Train* is a far more interesting and complex character than the hero, Guy Haines (Farley Granger), as Hitchcock himself noted (Truffaut, 1965/1986, p. 290). Consider also Otto Keller (O.E. Hasse), the murderer in *I Confess*, who makes a speech in a theatre auditorium before his death, proclaiming, with great pathos and tenderness, his love of his wife: 'It made me cry to see her work so hard', he tells the assembled audience, 'those poor hands, such beautiful hands.'

The films of D.W. Griffith were an important link between nineteenth-century literary and theatrical traditions, such as melodrama, and cinema. They provided Hitchcock with examples of how melodramatic elements could be woven into relatively sophisticated narrative forms which were still accessible to a mass audience. Hitchcock noted that Griffith's film-making was 'very clearly stated, you didn't have any difficulty following it' (in Gottlieb, 1997, p. 131). He also admired the suspense chases in films such as *Intolerance* (1916), *Birth of a Nation* (1915) and *Orphans of the Storm* (1921). Griffith's habit of 'crosscutting' (cutting backwards and forwards between two different scenes of action), was subsequently used in a more sophisticated fashion by Hitchcock on a number of occasions. At the climax of *Blackmail*, Hitchcock shows us the flight of the blackmailer, Tracy, pursued by the police, through the London streets and into the British museum. The footage of the chase is crosscut with shots of Alice sitting at home, completely distraught, yet almost motionless as she wrestles with her conscience over whether to turn herself in to the police and confess to murder. Both Alice and Tracy are in a state of panic but while the former's anxiety can be shown objectively in vigorous movements, Alice's has to be read through her facial expressions and what the audience must infer through knowledge of her situation.

In *Strangers on a Train* there is a suspenseful sequence in which the hero, a champion tennis player, has to finish his game before he can head off in pursuit of the killer. Here Hitchcock develops one of the main aspects of his suspense technique, keeping the audience suspended in narrative time, by using crosscutting. He cleverly retards the development of the narrative by cutting between the match and the killer, who is desperately trying to retrieve an incriminating cigarette lighter which he has managed to drop down a drain. The controlled action of the match is intercut with the frustrating attempts of the killer to retrieve the lighter. Only once the match has ended and the lighter retrieved can the narrative resume and the audience be allowed the pleasure of a satisfying dramatic climax. As Hitchcock explains, 'The camera, cutting alternately from the frenzied hurry of the tennis player to the slow operations of the enemy, creates a kind of counterpoint between the two kinds of movement' (in Gottlieb, 1997, p. 129).

Griffith saw the cinema as a popular art form and his innovations were welcomed by the film industry as they not only brought in a new and prosperous middle-class audience, but also placated the middle-class reformers who branded the cinema a vulgar and corrupting influence on the masses. This strategy of combining middle-class and mass culture appealed to Hitchcock for similar reasons. Obviously, it made business sense, for by extending the class appeal of movies Hitchcock maximised his audience and his box-office takings. Like Griffith, Hitchcock aimed for a fusion of the pictorial and spectacular with established literary source material. In a 1950 interview, Hitchcock cited John Buchan, John Galsworthy and Mrs Belloc Lowndes, popular and respected middlebrow writers, as important formative influences (Gottlieb, 1997, p. 131). Buchan was a Scottish mystery and adventure writer, whose 1915 novel *The Thirty-Nine Steps* was filmed by Hitchcock with great success in 1935. He enjoyed considerable popular success as a teller of well-crafted picaresque tales which tapped into a Boys' Own popular imperialism, one that Hitchcock would also exploit in *Secret Agent*, adapted from the 'Ashenden' stories of Somerset Maugham.

The 39 Steps provides a good example of the picaresque thriller, a genre that Hitchcock would successfully draw on in other films such as *Young and Innocent* (1937), *Foreign Correspondent* (1940), *Saboteur* (1942) and *North By Northwest* (1959). The picaresque thriller deals with the travails of a plucky and adventurous character, who, in a series of interlinked and colourful episodes, confronts various adversaries and life-threatening situations. Guy Cogeval notes:

> ... this theme of flight, to which Hitchcock continually returned – from The 39 Steps *(1935) through* Young and Innocent *(1937) and* Saboteur, *right up to* North by Northwest *(1959) – leads to a narrative in ballad form. The Hitchcockian hero is thus a rover, always escaping the police, society, himself or the 'clutches of the past'.*
>
> (Cogeval, 2001, p. 27)

The picaresque thriller is 'romantic' in the original meaning of the term, which is to say 'fanciful', and the protagonist is typically something of a rogue, like Roger Thornhill in *North by Northwest*. As previously pointed out, the picaresque narrative has its roots in ballad form: it is highly structured, with built-in rhythm and lends itself to musicality – a concept dear to Hitchcock in his own description of his work (see Chapter 3). The episodic structure of Buchan's novel exemplified Hitchcock's own approach to narrative construction. Films such as *The Man Who Knew Too Much*, *Saboteur*, *Foreign Correspondent* and *Torn Curtain* include spectacular chases which take the audience on a tour of striking locations. Pictorially, these films exploit the contrast between urban and pastoral settings, as in *The 39 Steps*, for instance, which moves from a bustling music hall in East London to a Highland setting and back again, or in *Foreign Correspondent* where an old windmill in the Dutch countryside provides a contrast to a crowded city square in Amsterdam. They also make use of well-known national monuments and stereotypical cultural settings such as Mount Rushmore in *North By Northwest*, the Statue of Liberty in *Saboteur* and the Lincoln Memorial in *Strangers on a Train*. Hitchcock discusses his exploitation of well-known national features in a discussion of *The Secret Agent* where he confesses that the climactic chase scene, which takes place in a chocolate factory, was designed to exploit another stereotypical aspect of the film's Swiss setting (Truffaut, 1965/1986, p. 142).

The early influence of Marie Belloc Lowndes also broadened out the range of Hitchcock's films and to some extent modernised them by suggesting how increased psychological depth could be given to stock characters, especially the heroine in peril. Eliot Stannard adapted Lowndes' best-selling novel, *The Lodger*, which had become a popular stage play, for Hitchcock in 1926. Belloc Lowndes strongly emphasises the lower-middle-class household as the locus of the story and foregrounds class relations from the start:

Had the Buntings been in a class lower than their own, had they belonged to that great company of human beings technically known as the poor, there would have been friendly neighbours ready to help them, and the same would have been the case had they belonged to the class of smug, well meaning, if unimaginative, folk whom they had spent so much of their lives in serving.

(Belloc Lowndes, 1996, p. 1)

In addition to her interest in the sympathetic portrayals of the lower middle class, Charles Barr notes her 'sensitive understanding of women's problems' her 'modern sensibility' and her interest in the psychology of crime all contrast strikingly with the masculine values and lack of interest in psychology found in Buchan's work (Barr, 1999, p. 15). Barr finds in this early contrast something of the tension between masculine and feminine worldviews in films such as *Vertigo* and *Rear Window* (1954), noted by feminist critics such as Tania Modleski and discussed at greater length in Chapter 5.

Daphne Du Maurier, author of the source novels for three of Hitchcock's films, *Jamaica Inn*, *Rebecca* and *The Birds*, was another writer strongly associated with feminine concerns. Although the first two were the choices of Charles Laughton and David Selznick respectively, it is nevertheless striking that Du Maurier emerges as his most filmed author. She was associated with the genre of the Gothic romance in which a suffering heroine endures emotional torture to emerge victorious in love. In *Rebecca*, a novel which enjoyed a great vogue among lower-middle-class readers, the central character, known only as 'she', is a mousy, suburban girl who has to find courage and self-respect in a snobby and intimidating upper-class milieu. The character of Mrs Danvers (Judith Anderson) is the very embodiment of the particular combination of evil, madness and perverse sexual obsession to be found in Gothic fiction such as Charlotte Brontë's *Jane Eyre* (1847), Robert Louis Stevenson's *Dr Jekyll and Mr Hyde* (1886) and Bram Stoker's *Dracula* (1897). Another Gothic theme, much favoured by Hitchcock, was that of *doubles* and *doubling*. *Strangers on a Train* is carefully structured to repeatedly invoke the idea of pairs, from the lengthy opening sequence in which we see only the contrasting pairs of shoes belonging to the two protagonists to the design on the cigarette lighter (a pair of crossed tennis racquets), which Guy is unfortunate enough to leave behind on the train near the start of the film. In the Gothic tradition, which goes on to include much expressionist art, the double is an externalisation of the dark, hidden and pathological side of an apparently normal human

Mrs Danvers (Judith Anderson) in *Rebecca* (1940) embodies a combination of madness, perverse sexuality and evil common to the gothic romance. © ABC Photography Archives.

nature. Thus in *Strangers on a Train*, the murderer Bruno (Robert Walker) is shown to be expressing a hidden murderous wish on the part of the hero, Guy (Farley Granger). Other examples of this doubling include Uncle Charlie and his niece, also called Charlie, in *Shadow of a Doubt* (1943). The niece identifies herself almost obsessively with her uncle, telling him 'we're not just uncle and niece . . . we're sort of like twins'. Manny Balestrero in *The Wrong Man*, falsely accused of robbery, also has a double in the real criminal, a man who looks very much like him. The overlap between their identities is reinforced by the dissolve from Manny's face to that of the robber where their images blend together.

Many of the darker aspects of Hitchcock's work, such as the theme of the double (*Doppelgänger*), are closely associated with German culture and, for Hitchcock, German films. Hitchcock saw German film-makers at work first-hand when he visited the UFA studios at Neubabelsberg. Here he observed Fritz Lang and F.W. Murnau, two of the best-known film-makers of the day, at work. While Lang had trained at university as an architect and Murnau was a scholar of art, philosophy and literature, Hitchcock had only his evening classes. Both Lang and Murnau went on to make films in Hollywood but Hitchcock would go on to eclipse both of them in both commercial success and, arguably, even in critical acclaim. S.S. Prawer has pointed out that Hitchcock shared with Lang an interest in transplanting 'the Romantic fantasies of the early German cinema, and its central *doppelgänger* image, into a realistic setting and an almost documentary story-line' (1980, p. 18). Hitchcock even borrowed actors from Lang, casting Bernard Göetzke in *The Mountain Eagle* (1926) after having seen him in Lang's *Destiny* (1921), while *Secret Agent* and *The Man Who Knew Too Much* (1934) starred Peter Lorre, newly famous from his portrayal of the child murderer in *M* (1931).

Hitchcock had already gained considerable exposure to German and Russian art cinema when, in 1925, a new organisation, the Film Society, was formed to provide British cinema-goers with access to foreign films. Its early membership included Ivor Montagu (an aristocrat and a Cambridge graduate), Adrian Brunel and Sidney Bernstein (both entrepreneurs in the film industry). Although Montagu stated that their aim was to popularise world cinema in the face of domination by American product, the Film Society constituted what Tom Ryall describes as a 'minority film culture'; it

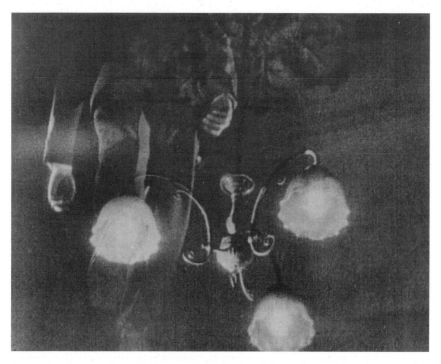

Shots like this one from *The Lodger* (1926), filmed through a specially constructed glass ceiling gave Hitchcock a reputation as an arty film maker working within a commercial film industry. Reproduced courtesy of itv plc (Granada International)/ LFI.

met with indifference or incomprehension from the cinema-going public and outright hostility from the industry itself, which felt threatened by its presence. According to Ryall, it was socially exclusive. He notes that '[t]he upper middle class university educated milieu of the minority film culture was quite at odds with the lower middle class background of shop keepers from which Hitchcock had come' (1996, p. 177). Through the Film Society Hitchcock made contacts with the film intelligentsia. He would later form a business partnership with Bernstein. However, at that time Bernstein was regarded with suspicion and resentment in the industry as he was not only a highly successful businessman, but also an intellectual. It would certainly appear as though Hitchcock had considerable artistic and intellectual aspirations in the 1920s and this became his early downfall when the release of Hitchcock's first three films was vetoed by the distributor C.M. Woolf. One element in Hitchcock's plight was his allegiance to Expressionism.

Several critics, including Robin Wood (1989) and John Belton (1980), have discussed the Expressionist element in Hitchcock's cinema and we know he had seen *The Cabinet of Dr Caligari* (1919), the most famous example of German Expressionist film-making. Expressionism was a movement in the arts which explored the emotional and philosophical truths hidden or denied in the society of the time. Expressionist film was often loaded with wilfully obscure symbols and metaphors that could be hard for the uninitiated to comprehend. In *The Cabinet of Dr Caligari* the use of visual effects, such as chiaroscuro lighting and stylised set design, was symbolic. As Lotte Eisner observes, 'these curves and slanting lines have a meaning which is decidedly metaphysical . . . what matters is to create states of anxiety and terror' (1969, p. 21). As someone who entered the film industry on the design side, Hitchcock quickly saw how effective these symbols were in creating a mood of disquiet. Corridors and staircases, shadows and mirrors, doubles and duality – these objects of fascination for the Expressionists were quickly integrated into the repertoire of Hitchcock's iconography, becoming repeated motifs, often used to exteriorise a character's subjective state.

The Lodger makes extensive use of Expressionist chiaroscuro lighting and long shadows, associated with fearful perceptions that the lodger is a murderer. These are particularly apparent in a scene where the lodger prepares to leave the house of the Bunting family late one night. Hitchcock crosscuts between the shadowy figure of the lodger making his way down the dark stairs and Mrs Bunting in her bedroom, anxiously aware of his every move. Similarly, there is a highly stylised sequence near the start of *Blackmail* where two policemen enter the lodgings of a criminal suspect. They make their way across a well-lit courtyard and into a dimly lit slum dwelling where they climb a dark staircase and pause outside the room of the suspect. The man sees the fractured reflection of the police in a mirror and Hitchcock cuts to a shot of his gun, lying by his bed. As the police enter we are given the two shots of the police with thick bars of light and shade across their faces, making them look far more sinister than the poor crook. In a related way, *Marnie* and *Vertigo* both use intense colour schemes to suggest interior states of mind. Maurice Yacowar notes, especially, the use of the staircase motif in films such as *The Lodger* and *Vertigo*, in which the shot is 'downward through a seeming spiral', and points out that '[t]he occasional round staircase, as in *The Pleasure Garden* and *Secret Agent*, also suggests a plunge through layers of the self' (Yacowar, 1986, p. 18).

The journey up or down a staircase is often the occasion for some of Hitchcock's most shocking and suspenseful scenes. He was fond of shooting staircases, describing them as 'very photogenic' (Samuels, 1972, p. 239). The first part of *Number Seventeen* (1932) is set in an old dark house whose centrepiece is a shadow-laden staircase where most of the action takes place. Likewise, there is the detective's death scene in *Psycho*, as he first climbs, then collapses backwards down the stairs in the Bates' house. Or Guy's ascent up the stairs to warn Bruno's father that his son is trying to kill him in *Strangers on a Train*, and the long, silent tracking shot down the stairs and out on to the street in *Frenzy*. Then there is the slow descent down the stairs made by Cary Grant and Ingrid Bergman in their attempt to escape from the Nazis in *Notorious* or the ascent of Johnnie Aysgarth (Cary Grant) up the stairs with a luminous glass of milk which might contain poison in *Suspicion*. In each case, the journey up or downstairs is one redolent of the Expressionist emphasis on anxious foreboding.

The Expressionist cinema was not the only type of German art cinema which affected Hitchcock. *The Last Laugh* (1924), directed by F.W. Murnau, often cited by Hitchcock as a great influence on him, is to be distinguished from Expressionism. It belongs under the heading of the *Kammerspiel* (literally, 'chamber play') film, involving the suppression of dialogue, a greatly enhanced sense of intimacy and the everyday. Technically and stylistically its great innovation was the *entfesselte Kamera* (the unchained camera) showcased by Murnau in *The Last Laugh*, where it roams freely throughout the sets and follows characters across great expanses of theatrical space. Freeing the camera up in this way also lent itself to a more inquisitive and even voyeuristic approach, where the camera follows characters around, peering into and out of doorways and window frames. Perhaps the most extreme instances of the unchained camera in Hitchcock's work are to be found in his fondness for extended crane shots. These are used in such films as *Young and Innocent*, *Notorious* and *Marnie*. In the first, the camera travels from the ceiling at the back of a huge ballroom, which it captures in extreme long shot, right through and keeps on going until it gives us an extreme close-up on the twitching eye of the drummer in the dance band. In the second, the camera begins a slow descent from the top of an imposing staircase in a grand house where a party is in progress, travels downwards until it comes to rest on an extreme close-up of a key clutched tightly in a hand. The long and slow crane shot down the grand staircase and right to the front door in *Marnie* is a deliberate echo of the one in *Notorious*. Both shots perform similar narrative functions, that is to disclose something in the middle of a bustling house party which will prove a threat to the heroine. In *Notorious* it is the stolen key to the wine cellar, which will ultimately lead to Alicia Huberman's (Ingrid Bergman) downfall. In *Marnie*, it is the appearance of Mr Strutt (Martin Gabel), a figure from Marnie Edgar's (Tippi Hedren) past, who threatens to expose her as a common thief as she is about to take on the mantle of a wealthy and sophisticated wife.

Such stylistic flourishes, many of them learnt from European art cinema in Hitchcock's early years, were not necessarily indulged in despite the commercial film industry. Far from being opposed to high art, the commercial British film industry during Hitchcock's apprentice years was struggling to appropriate elements from high and low culture in an effort to create a distinctive and imaginatively compelling product. Bergfelder (1996) has described the creative and cosmopolitan cultural exchanges which took place in the British film industry in the 1930s. This cross-pollination was very productive creatively, although some businessmen were nervous that overt 'artiness' would alienate audiences. When Hitchcock arrived in Hollywood, the influence of European art cinema movements had already made itself strongly felt through the influx of refugees, particularly from Germany.

While the influence of Expressionism and the *Kammerspielfilm* came from Germany, Hitchcock took from French art cinema some of the elements of 'Surrealism'. Surrealism was a movement which flourished in painting and poetry during the 1920s. Its emphasis on dreams or dream-like states and abnormal psychology was heavily influenced by Freud. In addition, the Surrealists viewed everyday objects as charged with meaning, much of it disturbing and threatening. As S.S. Prawer has pointed out, Hitchcock turns 'objects of our ordinary world and everyday use into agents of threat or betrayal' (1980, p. 130). Some examples would be: a bread knife in *Blackmail* which reminds the heroine of murder, a glass of milk which might be poisoned in *Suspicion*, a blood-stained doll in *Stage Fright*, and a trunk containing the strangled body of a young student which is used as a table top at a civilised cocktail party in *Rope* (1948). Writing in a French journal in 1960, Hitchcock spoke of the effect of Surrealism on his work, 'if only in the dream sequences and the sequences of the unreal in a number of my films' (in Gottlieb, 1997, p. 144). He cites Bunuel's *L'Age d'Or* (1930) and *Un Chien Andalou* (1928), René Clair's *Entr'acte* (1924), Jean Epstein's *La Chute de la Maison Usher* (1928), and Jean Cocteau's *Le Sang d'un Poete* (1930). Wollen (1997) has noted the similarities between André Breton's Surrealist novel *Nadja*, published in 1928, and *Vertigo*, especially the theme of *amour fou*, love which takes the form of a crazed obsession.

From the Russian revolutionary cinema, Hitchcock drew on the theory and practice of Sergei Eisenstein, the leading exponent of montage (editing). Montage can mean different things. In its original French meaning, it refers to film editing in general. However, the word is often used to denote a sequence of film in which editing techniques are used as a kind of special effect. Hitchcock emphasised the importance of montage and the effects that it was capable of generating in an interview with the film-maker Peter Bogdanovich: 'I think that montage is the essential thing in a motion picture', he remarked. 'Only montage has that power of audience suggestion. I'm very keen on that method of storytelling' (in Bogdanovich, 1997, p. 476).

Although theories of montage were developed within the art avant-garde, the Russian cinema also absorbed elements of popular culture. In his article on the 'Cinema of Attraction' (1986), Tom Gunning points out that the word 'attractions', used by Eisenstein in the 1920s to describe his method of montage, was derived from an enthusiasm for fairground attractions among modernist artists. He notes that this association between popular spectacular cinema and the cinema of attractions persists today in the films of Spielberg, Lucas and Coppola. This is the cinema as roller-coaster ride, and indeed Hitchcock has been credited by Linda Williams (1994) with providing us with the modern blueprint of such a cinema with *Psycho*. Commenting on the fairground scenes in *Strangers on a Train*, Prawer notes that 'roller-coasters, ghost trains, and freak-shows' proved attractive to the director 'because they too deal in *Angstlust*, in thrills that cause delight by playing on fear' (Prawer, 1980, p. 191). The fairground quality of Hitchcock's work was remarked on the *New York Post*'s review of *North By Northwest* which described it as 'a wonderful roller-coaster, merry-go-round of pure entertainment' (Kapsis, 1992, p. 56).

In the cinema of attractions the narrative exists mainly to hold together a series of set pieces. These spectacles are used to delight and astonish the audience through their skill and daring, to the extent that the characters and storylines may be quite unimportant. In Hitchcock's film *North By Northwest*, we see one of the clearest examples of a narrative that was largely created to facilitate a series of cinematic set pieces, the ideas for which were present in Hitchcock's mind long before there was a story or characters. The film's genesis was in an image that Hitchcock had in his mind of a chase across Mount Rushmore. He and his screenwriter Ernest Lehman worked out the story around that famous set piece, with Lehman declaring that he was going to write the ultimate Hitchcock film that could be built around a whole series of them. Hitchcock acknowledges that the film in itself was a reworking of *The 39 Steps*, another exercise in stringing together a series of set pieces (Domarchi and Douchet, 1959).

Gunning (1986) observes that the experience of fairgrounds and other forms of popular culture were found liberating by those members of the middle classes brought up on a diet of traditional culture who looked to redefine, sometimes radically, bourgeois values. Thus, it is possible to see that Hitchcock's problematic relation to traditional ideas of high and low art derives to some extent from his immersion in an early twentieth-century aspiration among film-makers and intellectuals to fuse the values of high art with those of fairground popular culture, partly in order to call into question accepted canons of taste. Although the terms 'highbrow', 'middlebrow' and 'lowbrow' are not as commonly used today as they were in Hitchcock's own lifetime, they nevertheless constituted widely recognised boundaries which were strongly underlined by class inequality. The American sociologist Herbert J. Gans has demonstrated the extent to which the terms 'highbrow', 'middlebrow' and 'lowbrow' correspond to the divisions between upper-middle, middle/lower-middle and working classes, expressing a 'socio-economic hierarchy' in cultural terms (Gans, 1999, p. vii). High culture, in particular, tends to be sharply restricted to those with a specific education and family background. Hitchcock's achievement in blending such a wide range of influences was not only cultural it was also social. This achievement represented a relatively rare instance of someone from the 'lower classes' successfully achieving a high degree of recognition among the upper-class intelligentsia while retaining a generalised popular appeal among the middle classes. In the next chapter Hitchcock's attempts to combine the roles of artist and showman will be examined in closer detail.

2 Authorship and reputation

Hitchcock is well known today as an *auteur* director, that is to say, in an industry where films are produced collectively, by many creative, business and technical personnel, his are thought to be exceptional in the degree of personal control that he exercised over them. But to what extent is it legitimate to consider Hitchcock the essential author of these industrially-produced films? What links are assumed between his work and his public images? To answer these questions it is helpful to acknowledge that there are at least two connotations attaching to Hitchcock's name: the artist and the celebrity. Of course, these need not be mutually exclusive and it is part of Hitchcock's importance that he manipulated his image carefully to maximise the impact of both.

First, consider the public images of Hitchcock, which were made up from the outset of representations authorised and supervised by Hitchcock and the public relations industry. This process began in earnest in 1930 with the formation of Hitchcock's own PR company, which helped to establish the idea of him as the jovial, rotund, black magician of the cinema. He gave interviews with numerous magazines, radio programmes and circulated large amounts of pre-publicity for each film, emphasising this eccentric persona, and he would use life-sized cardboard cut outs of his image in cinema entrances to promote his latest film. He sported his trademark business suit, bringing a stylised formality to all occasions, and wore it on the set, in the Swiss Alps for *Secret Agent* (1936), or in the sweltering heat of the Marrakesh sun when filming *The Man Who Knew Too Much* (1956). During the 1950s and 1960s he became instantly recognisable to the general public in America through his stage-managed appearances on his TV show, *Alfred Hitchcock Presents*.

These self-generated images are supplemented by 'highbrow' critical representations of Hitchcock as a great artist who tackles serious moral themes and whose films embody highly specific aesthetic features. These began in earnest in the 1950s with the journal *Cahiers du Cinéma* and carried on into the 1960s with the British journal *Movie* and a major retrospective of his work at the New York Museum of Modern Art in 1963, which was accompanied by a 48-page extended interview between the critic/director Peter Bogdanovich and Hitchcock. Then there are the unofficial, often negative representations of Hitchcock as a sinister manipulator which circulate with the aid of texts such as Donald Spoto's biography, *The Dark Side of Genius: The Life of Alfred Hitchcock* (1983). Spoto's book followed his earlier and far more favourable survey of Hitchcock's output, *The Art of Alfred Hitchcock* (1976), yet following the publication of this book, Spoto went through a period of disillusionment in which his previously idealised image Hitchcock was exchanged for an image of him as deceiving and duplicitous. Hitchcock emerges from the book as 'a tormented and mean spirited individual with the sexual immaturity of an adolescent' (Kapsis, 1992, p. 120). However, Spoto's determination to construct a particular image of Hitchcock ends up trying to fit a complex personality into the shape of a stereotyped tragic villain, a character from one of the films rather than a human being with the potential to be all manner of things to all manner of men and women.

The Dark Side of Genius contrasts with John Russell Taylor's earlier biography, *Hitch: The Life and Times of Alfred Hitchcock* (1978), a genial salute to the director by one of Hitchcock's friends. Taylor discusses some of the less flattering accounts of Hitchcock's behaviour, dismissing these largely as the expression of Hitchcock's sometimes cruel sense of fun. Russell Taylor's image of the jolly joker who sometimes went too far perhaps lets Hitchcock off too lightly while Spoto is constantly on the look out for sayings or doings which could be used as evidence of Hitchcock's cruel and sadistic nature.

A more productive approach is taken in *Hitchcock: The Making of a Reputation* (1992), by Robert A. Kapsis. Kapsis has made use of the concept of a *biographical legend* and used it as a means of surveying historically the various kinds of critical discourse which have been used to interpret Hitchcock's films. Ryall defines the biographical legend as 'the end product of a range of "historical" forces, which include the public utterances of the artist concerned together with a variety of discourses such as those of journalism, academic criticism, publicity and marketing' (Ryall, 1996, p. 6). The most interesting aspect of *The Making of a Reputation* is its documentation of Hitchcock's attempts to influence the ways in which critics constructed images of him and his films. The book reveals his highly advanced understanding of public relations and marketing processes mentioned earlier.

Kapsis provides evidence to show that Hitchcock took a keen interest in ideas, that he was aware of the various schools of film criticism and that he frequently and opportunistically geared his films to straddle the divide between highbrow intellectual culture and popular culture. From his early years in the film industry, Hitchcock repeatedly affirmed his understanding of the importance of film criticism to the success of his career, while at the same time retaining a dislike for the snobbery and elitism of the critics, who, he felt, misunderstood his films. In the 1920s Hitchcock was part of an informal discussion group called the Hate Club, so named because its members were irritated at the dismissive attitude towards film taken by much of the establishment. They were also irritated by the philistinism of the British film industry, which failed to appreciate the artistry of Russian and German cinema. In a discussion of *The Man Who Knew Too Much* (1934), Ivor Montagu, a fellow member of the Hate Club, remembers Hitchcock remarking:

> *You're not making [a film] for the public because by the time the public*
> *sees it it doesn't really matter what happens to it. The main thing is that*
> *the public will never see it if the distributor doesn't like it. Are you making it*
> *for the Press? He decided that you were making it for the Press, and the trade*
> *was quite right in smelling this out and feeling that he was trying to get good*
> *notices.*
>
> *(Montagu, 1972, p. 80)*

Hitchcock went to considerable lengths to engineer his public image and to 'educate' both audiences and critics in what to expect from a Hitchcock film from an early stage in his career (Kapsis, 1992). He actively promoted the idea of the director as artist, breaking new ground in the medium, and as early as 1927 *The Bioscope*, a trade journal, reviewed *Downhill* (1927) by pointing out that 'the selling angle is the name of Hitchcock'.

In a letter to the *London Evening News*, Hitchcock compares the work of the film director to that of a novelist:

> *It is obvious that what we must strive for at once is the way to use these film*
> *nouns and verbs as cunningly as do the great novelist and the great dramatist,*
> *to achieve certain moods and effects on an audience. . . . When moving*
> *pictures are really artistic they will be created entirely by one man.*
>
> *(Gottlieb, 1997, pp. 166–7)*

However, Kapsis does not see such interventions as evidence of Hitchcock's egomania, as Spoto seems to suggest. Instead, 'Hitchcock's early efforts at self-promotion . . . were part of standard European and American industrial and advertising practices. What was novel about Hitchcock is that he became successful at self-promotion while so many others who also tried this tactic failed' (Kapsis, 1992, p. 17).

Kapsis also notes that 'Throughout the 1940s Hitchcock continued his practice of including unusual shots or sequences in his films for their calculated effect on the more serious critics' (1992, p. 25). An example of this would be the use of Surrealist Salvador Dali's designs in *Spellbound* (1945), the name of the artist alone guaranteeing publicity in more upmarket publications. Another example would be *Foreign Correspondent* (1940). Hitchcock points out to Truffaut, 'there were a lot of ideas in that picture', including a highly artistic shot of a windmill (used as a hideout for spies) whose sails move against the direction of the wind and a stylised shooting sequence which features a chase through a crowd under a sea of black umbrellas in torrential rain (1965/1986, p. 188). The trailer for *Frenzy* (1972) showcases a particularly striking and mysterious long shot of Hetty Porter (Billie Whitelaw) staring down from the balcony of an apartment block as a foretaste of Hitchcock's cinematic virtuosity.

However, Hitchcock's construction of himself and his work could sometimes backfire, especially when his films somehow challenged expectations encouraged by his persona. Bold and adventurous films such as *The Wrong Man* (1957), a true story which ventured into a bleakly realistic, semi-documentary style and *Vertigo* (1957), a deeply personal and stylised drama which had a tragic ending were both comparative failures. Critics rounded on the films for lacking the 'Hitchcock touch' and the public, undoubtedly influenced by reviews and word of mouth, stayed away. Hitchcock's error was to have tackled very serious subjects in artistic fashion, with little of his trademark humour. Furthermore, although *The Wrong Man* has its hero triumph at the end, the view of society and human relationships in both this film and in *Vertigo* is exceptionally bleak and pessimistic.

The television series, *Alfred Hitchcock Presents*, which started in 1955 was, however, an immediate success, making Hitchcock the most famous and instantly recognisable of all film directors. He told a journalist, 'Before TV, I'd get about a dozen letters a week. Now it's several hundred' (in Kapsis, 1992, p. 34). His name and physical presence at the start of each show identified him so closely with the series that he created the impression of having written and directed all the episodes, whereas he wrote none of them and directed only 15 of the 268 episodes. According to one disgruntled script writer, Hitchcock's fan mail showed that 'there were hundreds and maybe thousands of viewers out there who believed that Alfred Hitchcock was the author of the tales he told. So much for credits' (in Kapsis, 1992, p. 32). Hitchcock began each programme with his theme tune (Gounod's 'Funeral March of a Marionette'), followed by his trademark silhouette and finally his familiar greeting: 'Good evening, I am Alfred Hitchcock.' These were simple, but very effective exercises in branding, the process whereby a simple and easily recognisable figure,

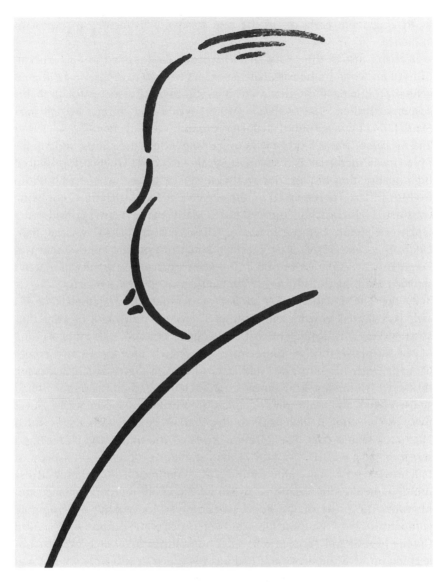

This simple sketch, devised by Hitchcock himself, was one of the ways in which he was able to transform himself into a successful and easily recognisable brand. Courtesy of Patricia H. O'Connell and Leland H. Faust, Trustees of the Alfred J. Hitchcock Trust.

such as a logo or other sign, becomes invested with value and meaning for the consumer. And, of course, the figure most associated with Hitchcock's product was the image of his round body. This was carried over into his later films where Hitchcock's already established fleeting appearances in his own films became so eagerly anticipated by audiences that he took to making them early on in the film to avoid distracting an expectant audience.

It wasn't just in the 1950s that Hitchcock confounded public expectations of his work. In the past, Hitchcock had worked in a variety of different genres producing films that were less commercially successful than his suspense thrillers. *The Manxman* (1929) was a melodrama; *Mr and Mrs Smith* (1941) was an out of character romantic comedy; *Bon Voyage* (1944) and *Adventure Malgache* (1944) were wartime propaganda films; and *Marnie* (1964) was marketed as a sex mystery. In each case, Hitchcock produced high-quality films but lost out on the steady audience that he had built up for his thrillers. He remarked on the negative effect of such films not being considered 'Hitchcock pictures': '*Mr and Mrs Smith* . . . wasn't considered a Hitchcock picture because it had no chase. *Lifeboat* (1944) was another. *Under Capricorn* (1949) wasn't really a Hitchcock picture either – that was Bergman. . . . People go to one of my films expecting a thriller and aren't satisfied until the thrill turns up' (in Gottlieb, 1997, pp. 132–3).

By the 1960s, Hitchcock's success at defining the parameters of his style had started to work against him. There was much talk of films out-Hitchcocking Hitchcock. The first challenge to Hitchcock's throne, as King of the suspense thriller, came from the French director Henri-Georges Clouzot, with his film *Les Diaboliques* (1954), a clever Hitchcock-esque thriller which made a strong impression on critics and on the public. It had stylised black and white photography, brooding atmosphere and a clever twist at the end. It also had an inspired marketing campaign, which Hitchcock would later plagiarise for *Psycho*. Furthermore, the James Bond series, starting with *Dr No* (1962), had started to capitalise on aspects of Hitchcock's now successful formula of glamorous stars, chases across multiple picturesque locations, stylish art direction, murder, romance and humour. The onset of the Bond series saw critics making unfavourable comparisons between these films and Hitchcock's later output, such as *Torn Curtain* (1966) and *Topaz* (1969), with accusations that Hitchcock was not keeping up with the times and had lost his touch. It was only the last two films, *Frenzy* and *Family Plot* (1976), that were thought to have regained the legendary 'Hitchcock touch', the supposedly characteristic blend of humour, suspense, sophistication, thrills, a light touch and dark subject matter. Part of Hitchcock's problem, especially with subtle and original films such as *Vertigo*, lay with the fact that he had been so successful in defining his image that anything which departed too much from people's expectations of a 'Hitchcock film' was met with confusion and disappointment.

Like any other commercial film-maker, Hitchcock's name was expected to deliver customer satisfaction; yet he often wanted to stretch his talents beyond the confines of what the audience would find easily digestible.

This he quite frequently did, hoping that he could carry the audience with him. Films such as *The Lodger* (1926), *Rope* (1948), *Under Capricorn* (1949) and *The Birds* (1963) show Hitchcock challenging the existing boundaries of the feature film and what the audience expects of it. Hitchcock's willingness to defy convention (even if the unintended result was audience disapproval) is manifest, for instance, in his decision to open *Stage Fright* (1950) with a lying flashback or to show the young child blown up by a bomb on a bus in *Sabotage* (1936).

This 'pioneering' aspect of Hitchcock's films gives rise to the critical discourse of the *auteur*, the film artist *par excellence*. As mentioned earlier, this discourse on Hitchcock started out life in the pages of *Cahiers du Cinéma*, a journal launched in 1951 by a group of young critics, film-makers and enthusiasts led by André Bazin. Bazin had argued that a camera does not simply record reality. Rather, in the hands of certain exceptional film-makers, cinema is reality filtered through the consciousness of an artist whose own thoughts and feelings about what they film can resonate deeply with the audience. This idea is also illustrated in Alexandre Astruc's 1948 essay, 'The Birth of a New Avant Garde: Le Camera Stylo', which argued that the great director uses the camera to 'write', leaving an indelible personal signature on the film, particularly its mise-en-scène, that is, the director's use of lighting, set design, costumes and movement within the frame. Hitchcock became one of the first and most enduring test cases for this new approach to cinema and, in turn, it influenced his own view of his work. So much so, in fact, that screenwriter Albert Goldman has argued that it was 'the *auteur* theory that ruined him – or at least his belief in it' (1996, p. 105).

Central to any consideration of Hitchcock as an *auteur* is this concept of mise-en-scène, which has been defined as 'the contents of the frame and the way they are organised' (Gibbs, 2002, p. 5). The critics writing for *Cahiers du Cinéma* wanted to draw attention to the sophisticated visual language in Hitchcock's films, and encouraged the detailed observation of camera placements, lighting, colour, costume, etc. Hitchcock's inspired use of mise-en-scène can be seen in the opening of *Strangers on a Train* (1950), where for the first few minutes of the film, the camera shows us only the legs and shoes of two men as they get out of separate taxis and make their way on to a train. The aim of the sequence is to establish differences (and connections) between the two main characters through their dress sense: the owner of the first pair of feet is Bruno Anthony (Robert Walker), a charming psychopath, who sports a pair of loud two-tone shoes. The camera cuts to the second pair of feet, which belong to Guy Haines (Farley Granger), a conservatively dressed, upwardly mobile tennis star. Both men are smartly dressed, but Bruno's snazzy taste in footwear has already marked him out as the more interesting character compared to the sane, respectable but rather dull Guy. This means of immediately delineating character relies on none of the traditional verbal techniques employed in drama and the novel, but on a manipulation of a *visual* language.

Likewise, *Psycho* (1960) opens on an aerial view of a city (Phoenix, Arizona – shown from the 'God's eye view' again) before moving in closer, in a series of dissolves. We see a high-rise hotel and the camera seems to enter one of the rooms under a crack in the open hotel window. Once inside the camera looks around the room and appears to sit down in a chair to observe the clandestine sexual liaison between a couple in their early thirties, Sam Loomis (John Gavin) and Marion Crane (Janet Leigh). Their desperation has driven them to meeting in hotel rooms during Marion's lunch hour. Martin Scorsese has noted that what makes Hitchcock's use of the camera so disturbing in *Psycho* is 'the feeling that there's another person in the room, making a ghostly inventory of every object, every move' (Scorsese, 1999, p. 36).

Later in the same film, during the parlour scene where Marion and Norman (Anthony Perkins) talk at some length, the mise-en-scène communicates a number of things to the audience. First, the décor in Norman's parlour is strongly evocative of a bygone era. The furnishings are clearly Norman's mother's and, in the context of the story, emphasise the hold which the past still exerts over him. Then there are the stuffed birds of which Hitchcock remarks, 'they were like symbols'. The stuffed owl in flight mounted on the wall represented, to Hitchcock, the masochistic pleasure which Norman took in being watched while doing wrong (Truffaut, 1986, p. 434). The camera set-ups during the scene also register a shift during the conversation. In the first half of the scene, the camera views Norman and Marion at eye level and alternates medium close-ups of them conversing. However, the dynamic changes as conversation turns to Norman's mother. 'You know', says Marion, 'if anyone ever talked to me the way I heard . . .', at this point the camera cuts to Norman, shot from below, as he leans forward, giving the audience a close-up of his face in one corner of the frame with the stuffed owl in flight gazing down on both of them in the other corner. Marion's voice continues over the image of Norman as his smile fades: '. . . the way she spoke to you . . .' The camera cuts back to Marion, framing her face more closely, and then back to Norman, once again, shot from below. There follows an extended sequence of views of Marion shot, as before, at eye level but closer in alternating with shots of Norman shot from below, framed by the stuffed birds on the wall. The shift marks the moment when Norman's pathological side is engaged through the criticisms of his mother. From here on, what is made clear in rational terms to the audience through the dialogue (that is, that he has a distorted view of reality and that his relationship with his mother is neurotic) is underscored emotionally by the unsettling camera angles used to film him. The eerie and atmospheric presence of the birds of prey in the frame also serve as a portent of Norman's voyeurism and his association with terror, thus contributing to the suspense felt by the audience.

In films such as *Rear Window* (1954), *Rope* and *Psycho*, the camera becomes a specialised tool for surveilling and spying – a high-tech prosthesis for Hitchcock, the coolly fascinated, analytical voyeur. In these films the camera inquisitively follows the characters around and watches through windows, door frames and spy holes, often making us aware of its presence on the set. But other mise-en-scène factors, such as costume, colour and lighting, were also used in Hitchcock's films to great effect. For *The Trouble with Harry* (1955), Hitchcock had leaves painted different colours and pinned to artificial trees in the studio to create his own version of autumn in Vermont. *Vertigo*, on the other hand, emphasises the colours red and green. The interior of Ernie's restaurant, where a sweeping, virtuoso long take introduces Madeleine/Judy (Kim Novak), is a sumptuous deep red (carrying connotations of passion, blood and danger). This colour is echoed in the way that the camera picks out red flowers throughout the film, by red flashes in Scottie's dream and a red filter on the dissolve which opens Judy's flashback to her part in the murder of Gavin Elster's (Tom Helmore) wife. The colour green is also used repeatedly throughout the film. Examples include Madeleine/Judy's dresses and the green neon light outside the Empire Hotel which lights up Judy's room, lending her a ghostly green glow at times.

In several of the sets on *Psycho* and *Vertigo*, Hitchcock had the art director place mirrors, to create a mysterious extra perspective on the action. One of Hitchcock's most striking single shots is that of Scottie peeping through a crack in a door frame to observe Madeleine/Judy in a flower shop. The audience can see Stewart (unseen by Madeleine/Judy) on one side of the frame gazing at her, while on the other side of the frame she is walking in his direction and looking straight at the camera. This is possible because we are looking at her image reflected in a mirror next to the door, behind which Scottie is hiding. The framing has the effect of looking in on two worlds simultaneously. First, that of the flower shop, a feminine space, which has colour, light and social activity. The other world is the dark, furtive and alienated masculine world of the private detective looking in on the first world with a keen yearning. The artistic composition of the image is strikingly similar to a Pre-Raphaelite painting, *The Long Engagement* by Arthur Hughes, in which a cleric wearing dark, drab clothing, his face in shadow, is shown with a radiant young woman surrounded by bright flowers. It is quite possible that Hitchcock knew of the painting.

In addition to their mise-en-scène, Hitchcock's films are notable for their use of editing, which he referred to as montage. Editing techniques such as cuts, dissolves, superimpositions and wipes can be used to create the effect of an intense experience, the rapid passing of time, or the movement from scene to scene in a stylish and sometimes memorable fashion. The montage of cuts in the *Psycho* shower scene or the bird attack at the gas station in *The Birds* are both examples of the ways in which Hitchcock employed editing to intensify the experience of horror. Sometimes Hitchcock used editing to convey the state of mind of a protagonist going through an intense subjective experience (known as a *vorkapich* montage). The dreamlike montage of shots in *Blackmail* (1929) as the confused and disorientated Alice (Anny Ondra) wanders the streets of London after having killed a man by accident are an example of such a technique. The sequence begins as Alice White leaves the apartment of the man she has murdered during a struggle in which he tries to rape her. As she wanders the streets, transparent images of passers-by are transposed on to the image of Alice, indicating her self-absorption. The camera shows a close-up of a traffic policeman with his arm outstretched. It then cuts to a close-up of Alice's face, then back to the policeman's arm and back to Alice again. Then there is a subjective insert of the murdered man's arm lying outstretched as she left it, poking from behind a curtain. Alice crosses the street and makes her way through a crowd of theatre-goers when she looks up and the camera cuts to neon street signs ahead. In a close-up shot, Alice looks over to an ad for Gordon's London Gin, which promotes its white purity. (There is some irony here as Alice's surname is White.) There is then a close-up of Alice's face followed by a close-up of an animated cocktail shaker flickering up and down on the sign. Then there is a dissolve to an imagined image of a neon hand holding a knife in place of the cocktail shaker, flickering up and down in a stabbing motion. The effect of the shots in sequence is to demonstrate the intensity of feeling which Alice is experiencing. But perhaps more importantly it exists to foster a closer identification between Alice and the audience so that her subsequent difficulties in verbally communicating register the insensitivity of those around her, particularly her boyfriend, Frank.

Another type of montage, *intellectual* montage, is used in Hitchcock's films to plant an image in the mind of the audience which isn't necessarily on the screen. Throughout the shower scene in *Psycho*, Hitchcock took extreme care to avoid showing the knife touching the body and no stab wounds are shown. In a supremely effective display of Eisenstein's principle of intellectual montage, the knife entering Marion's flesh and the wounds and the blood coming from them are all in the imagination of the audience. The stabbing features 70 cuts made in 45 seconds and took a week to edit. Typically, for Hitchcock, this most intellectual exercise is employed to create the most visceral impact on the audience.

Likewise the crop duster sequence in *North By Northwest* (1959) employs a dense assemblage of shots (130 in a 9-minute sequence) to convey suspense as the hero, Roger O. Thornhill (Cary Grant), is deposited by a bus in the middle of deserted cornfields. The audience knows that he has arranged to meet a strange double, and that his life may be in danger, but they do not yet know who the man is or what form of danger Thornhill is in. Hitchcock builds the suspense by alternating shots of Thornhill looking around at the bus stop with point of view shots of the deserted road, then a distant aeroplane in the sky, then a car coming towards him which drives past, then another car, which also drives straight past him. Another car drives up and drops off a man in a suit and hat who stands and waits on the other side of the road. Hitchcock shows us each man scrutinising the other by cutting back and forth between them, in shot/reverse shot fashion. Finally, Thornhill crosses over to question the man who, it turns out, is merely waiting for a bus. It is not until the bus arrives and collects the other man that Thornhill realises it is the plane he has to fear. The attack of the crop duster plane is filmed using a mixture of close-ups of Thornhill ducking the plane and crouching in the corn stalks, and long shots of the plane circling in the sky above him. Luc Moullet, a contributor to *Cahiers du Cinéma*, wrote of the scene that 'it serves as a definition of Hitchcock's art' (in Naremore, 1993, p. 196). However, it's worth remembering that most of the scene was conceived in detail by the script writer Ernest Lehman, who was trying to encapsulate Hitchcock's cinematic approach.

It has been noted that Hitchcock's editing style obsessively returns to the theme of looking and being looked at. As Naremore puts it:

> He became the cinema's most famous exponent of a kind of psychological editing, in which the meaning of a sequence derives from careful alternations between the 'inner' and the 'outer' points of view. . . . Hitchcock's technique . . . actually depends upon a careful manipulation of two formal extremes: the purely subjective shot/reverse shot, focalized through a character; and the purely objective shot, often positioned from a 'bird's eye' vantage, looking down on a scene.
>
> (Naremore, 1993, p. 13)

Often, neither the character nor the audience can see the person who is looking. Thornhill cannot see the drivers of the cars which come towards him and then drive away, nor can he see who is piloting the plane. At other times, the camera looks down at the scene from a high angle with an all-knowing objectivity – a kind of God's eye view. The crop duster episode opens with one such high angle shot surveying the landscape and showing the arrival of Thornhill. The opening of *Psycho* has the camera hovering in the air over the city of Phoenix. As Durgnat suggests, 'the camera's destination suggests a secret event astir that we earthbound creatures can't see but that somebody up there can' (Durgnat, 2002, p. 23). Later in the film, when detective Arbogast (Martin Balsam) goes back into the Bates' house to investigate further, he is brutally struck down by 'mother' at the top of the stairs. The murder act was shot from a high angle which was partly to conceal the face of Arbogast's attacker and partly so Hitchcock could contrast the image of Arbogast's small figure with the subsequent extreme close-up of his bloody face. However, the scene also gains an eerie quality from the fact that the stabbing is seen from a point of view that no ordinary human being would physically occupy. This sequence has also been read as a punning reference to a montaged sequence in Eisenstein's *Battleship Potemkin* (1925) when the camera cuts from a soldier with a sabre to a close-up of a woman's bloodied face.

Throughout Hitchcock's work there is the continued recognition that editing is crucial to generate specific meanings. *The Birds* contains several sequences in which Hitchcock's use of editing is used especially to explore the dynamics of seeing and being seen. In the Bodega Bay sequence where Melanie Daniels takes a boat back from the residence of Mitch Brenner, Hitchcock cuts backwards and forwards repeatedly between Melanie and Mitch, as first Melanie sees Mitch unseen, and then they watch each other. The scene builds up a tension which culminates in a single gull swooping out of the sky to attack Melanie. The sequence has famously been analysed in great detail by Raymond Bellour (2000). In a later sequence which begins inside a café, the camera cuts between shots of the birds swooping down to attack townsfolk outside with reaction shots of Melanie, who is then stuck inside a phone booth while trying to raise help. The editing draws attention to a reversal of roles as Melanie is now trapped in a cage while the birds are free to circle around her.

So Hitchcock's command of editing and mise-en-scène seem to mark him out as an *auteur*, but how does the wider artistry of Hitchcock's films fit in with the notion of the *auteur* in general? Perhaps the most influential and decisive intervention over the *auteurship* debate was a book by Andrew Sarris, called *The American Cinema* (1968). In this book, Sarris created a 'pantheon' of great directors, ranking them in order of greatness. Hitchcock was placed in the first rank, along with Ford, Welles, Griffith, Hawks, Lang and Renoir. Sarris based his study on the French *politique des auteurs* but controversially translated this as 'the *auteur theory*'. The problem here is that the French word '*politique*' does not mean 'theory' and is better rendered as 'policy'. The difference is crucial, as 'the *auteur* theory' implies a claim that great films come about solely because of great directors. The *'auteur* policy' however, is a much less dogmatic and qualified term, indicating that the French critics were pursuing a certain strategy at that moment in order to achieve certain immediate goals. These included the perceived need to divert attention away from the script as the source of value in a film in an era when the art of the director was little understood or appreciated.

In spite of the undoubted merits of Sarris's book, the consequence of the success of *The American Cinema* enabled a dogmatic kind of film criticism to set in, which concentrated on Hitchcock to the damaging exclusion of the creative contributions of other members of the film-making team, and also the industrial conditions in which the film was produced. 'Hitchcock's films' were the products of different companies (among them Gainsborough, Gaumont, BIP, Selznick International, RKO, MGM, Paramount, Warner Brothers, Universal and his own Transatlantic Films), who employed the director on a salary along with teams of people to assist him. Unlike most fine artists, Hitchcock could not always choose his own projects. The idea to make several of the films (from those made in the 1930s while he was under contract with BIP to *Topaz*, made in 1969) came from studio executives, who commissioned the (sometimes reluctant) director to make the film. Similarly, some of Hitchcock's most cherished projects were vetoed by the studios. Even at the height of his success, Hitchcock complained that Universal Pictures had put a clause in his contract expressly forbidding him to make the story which had most inspired him, J.M. Barrie's *Mary Rose* (Mogg, 1999, p. 182). The *auteur* theory, however, tended to assume that a director's vision was all that really mattered, the politics of the industry were not considered to be of much interest or importance.

Another major consequence of *The American Cinema* was to encourage a generation of directors to see themselves as the true stars of their films. Hitchcock had led the way by putting his name in large print on the publicity material for his films, sometimes larger than that of his stars. Now directors such as Francis Coppola, Steven Spielberg, George Lucas and Brian De Palma began to market themselves as successful brand names.

Hitchcock's self-awareness of his artistry's value as a brand was clearly implicit in his own approach to his role as a film director. In a way, he is a prototype for the practice that Andy Warhol claims to have invented: *art/business and business/art*, that is to say disregarding the conventional separation of businessman and artist, treating business as a kind of art and art as a business. Warhol writes, 'being good in business is the most fascinating kind of art . . . making money is art and working is art and good business is the best kind of art' (1976, p. 88). Warhol chose Hitchcock

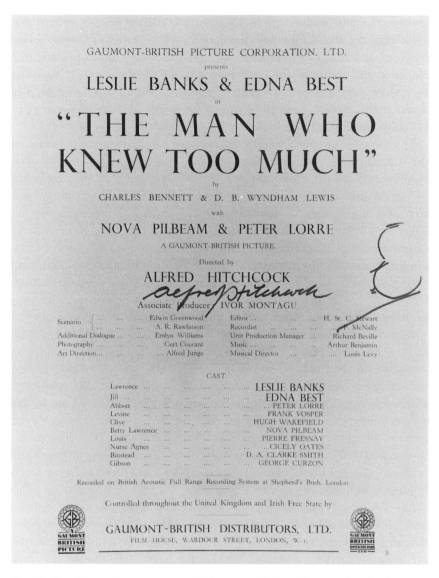

The Hitchcock branding strategy: publicity material from the press book of
The Man Who Knew Too Much (1934) with the director's signature and 'logo'.
Courtesy of Patricia H. O'Connell and Leland H. Faust, Trustees of the Alfred J.
Hitchcock Trust.

for a feature in his *Interview* magazine in 1974, where they were photo-
graphed chatting away animatedly. Perhaps they were closer in spirit
than they might look at first sight. Playwright Michael Eaton seems to have
thought so, for in 2000 he wrote a play called *Drella and the Macguffin*,
staging an imaginary encounter between the two men which draws out

their overlapping concerns. However, in another way the comparison is misleading: Hitchcock's art/business was far more collaborative than individual. Furthermore, because his work was so capital intensive, it was much more directly mediated by the demands of studio executives and audiences. One area in which this becomes explicit is the implementation of imagery and stylistic devices in his films, especially his use of sound.

3 Fascinating design: image, nothingness, sound and silence

'Isn't it a fascinating design. One could study it forever', Hitchcock remarked to Truffaut of *Strangers on a Train* (1950) (in Truffaut, 1965/1986, p. 185). Hitchcock's tendency to think of his films in terms of patterns of elements may be due to his early training in graphic design, which sharpened his sense of visual style, a feature noted by Martin Scorsese (1999, p. 13). Of directing *The Birds* (1963), Hitchcock said: 'It's just like designing composition in a painting. Or a balance of colours. There is nothing accidental, there should never be anything accidental about these things' (in Gottlieb, 1997, p. 294). His approach to the story material was analytical and self-conscious: 'The screen ought to speak its own language', he wrote, 'and it can't do that unless it treats an acted scene as a piece of raw material which must be broken up, taken to bits, before it can be woven into an expressive visual pattern' (in Gottlieb, 1997, p. 256).

However, at other times he was equally fond of comparing himself to a musician. He told Bogdanovich that 'Pure cinema is complementary pieces of film put together, like notes of music make a melody' (in Bogdanovich, 1997, p. 522). On yet another occasion he described cinema as 'the orchestration of shots' (in Samuels, 1972, p. 234). At such times, Hitchcock compared himself to a fine artist rather than a technician or a business-man. Much of the effect of Hitchcock's cinema lies in its awareness of the power of composition, in which visual and sonic elements achieve an indis-soluble blend.

Hitchcock could give the impression that formal design was all he cared about, as in these remarks made about *Psycho* (1960):

> *I don't care about the subject matter: I don't care about the acting; but I do care about the pieces of film and the photography and the soundtrack and all the technical ingredients that made the audience scream.*
>
> *(in Truffaut, 1965/1986, p. 434)*

For this reason, Hitchcock is sometimes treated as a modernist artist who rigorously explores form. William Rothman, author of *Hitchcock: The Murderous Gaze*, claims: 'If there is a modernist cinema . . . it begins with Hitchcock, in whose work film attains a modern self-consciousness' (1982, p. 6). The critic Peter Wollen agrees that Hitchcock should be compared with the great modernist artists and thinkers: 'I regard Hitchcock as one of the great artists of the twentieth century, genuinely on a par with Stravinsky or Kafka. . . . Hitchcock's preoccupation with the look or the gaze . . . can perfectly well be seen in conjunction with Sartre's concerns' (Wollen, 1998, p. 157). The director's self-conscious, analytical formalism has much in common with modernist art movements, particularly Russian Constructivism, which aimed at new ways of observing the world using the technology of the 'camera eye'. The eye of the camera was considered by Russian film-makers such as Dziga Vertov to be capable of revealing the world in a more scientific and truthful way than the human eye. Hitchcock's formalism suggests an objective, yet enquiring gaze at the world, frequently manifesting a distanced, disengaged and ironic view of events. The sequences from *The Birds* and *North by Northwest* (1959) discussed in the previous chapter provide two examples.

Many writers have singled out Hitchcock's manipulation of form as his greatest achievement. In 1957 Eric Rohmer and Claude Chabrol wrote that 'Hitchcock is one of the greatest *inventors of form* in the entire history of cinema . . . an entire moral universe has been elaborated on the basis of this form and by its very rigour. In Hitchcock's work form does not embellish content, it creates it. All of Hitchcock's work can be summed up in this formula' (Rohmer and Chabrol, 1957/1992, p. 152). Rothman asserts that in Hitchcock's films 'the camera performs gestures that have the force of claims, demonstrations, arguments' (1999, p. 31). Two critics associated with the British journal *Movie* in the early 1960s succeeded in arguing persuasively that the greatness of Hitchcock's films could only be appreciated through rigorous formal analysis. In early issues of *Movie* Ian Cameron discussed *The Man Who Knew Too Much* (1956) while V.F. Perkins looked at *Rope* (1948) using detailed descriptions of what forms the director is creating on the screen and analysing what effects he achieves. The same approach was extended further in Robin Wood's book, *Hitchcock's Films*, first published in 1965. The aim of such analysis was to detect repeated themes and motifs, both within the films and between them. For instance, the spiral motif in *Vertigo* (1957), which appears in the title sequence, in the hairstyle of Madeleine Elster, the staircase in the Church, the rings in the trunk of the Sequoia trees, and in Scottie's dream sequence. Along with detailed descriptions of the mise-en-scène went critical interpretation, designed to draw out latent subtexts within the films. Since the publication of Wood's breakthrough work, close textual interpretation has dominated the academic study of Hitchcock's films, often giving short shrift to Hitchcock's own views and rarely questioning the validity of Freudian theory. It is only in the last decade or so that researchers such as Gottlieb (1997 and 2000), Rebello (1990), Krohn (2000) and Kapsis (1992) have brought out the importance of the films' commercial origins along with their production and reception histories, thereby offering an important supplement to text-centred approaches. Either way, there is little doubt that the films are not superficial cultural products or that Hitchcock and his collaborators traded in the sort of depth and complexity that few other entertainers are interested in. The lightness of touch displayed by Hitchcock in his treatment of formal composition and its relationship to meaning can be shown through a consideration of the importance of 'nothings', sounds and silences in the films.

If 'things' in Hitchcock's films are often endowed with deep significance by critics and fans alike, 'nothings' can also be read as highly significant. Apropos of his treatment of form, Truffaut remarks to Hitchcock, 'emptiness has a magnetic appeal for you', a point with which the director agrees (1965/1986, p. 493). There is a focus on nothingness and emptiness in some currents in Eastern thought which were becoming well known in Hitchcock's time through the popularity of Existentialism. In Mahayana Buddhism there is a word *sunyata*, meaning absolute nothingness. *Sunyata* is a Sanskrit word which also has connotations of swollen-ness (appropriately enough for Hitchcock, given his figure) or pregnancy, and it is written as '0' (as in zero). Nothingness is pregnant with meaning and is the origin of all creativity. In Hitchcock's films it is nothingness, emptiness and, crucially, silence, which provide some of the richest possibilities to create sense and emotion.

This inevitably leads on to consideration of the MacGuffin, which Hitchcock describes as 'something that the characters worry about but the audience does not' (Bogdanovich, 1997, p. 502). The MacGuffin (a term coined by Hitchcock's collaborator at Gaumont British, Angus MacPhail) is used as a device around which to structure events. It appears to motivate people and events in the narrative, yet Hitchcock claims it is irrelevant. According to Hitchcock, it might be 'to steal a plan or documents, or discover a secret, it doesn't matter what it is' (in Truffaut, 1965/1986, p. 192). Examples include the secret plans held in Mr Memory's head in *The 39 Steps* (1935), the secret treaty clause in *Foreign Correspondent* (1940), the uranium ore hidden in wine bottles in *Notorious* (1946) and the stolen $40,000 in *Psycho*.

Hitchcock once claimed that the microfilm hidden inside a small statue in *North By Northwest* was his greatest MacGuffin, proudly proclaiming it

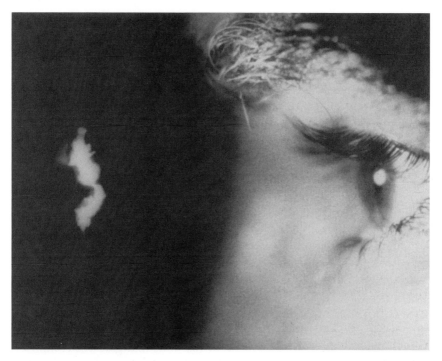

Norman Bates (Anthony Perkins) watches Marion Crane (Janet Leigh) undress through a spyhole in *Psycho* (1960). Note the simple, graphic impact of the shot. Courtesy of Universal Studios Licensing LLLP.

'the emptiest, most non-existent . . . the MacGuffin has been boiled down to its purest expression: nothing at all' (in Truffaut, 1965/1986, p. 195). According to Truffaut, Hitchcock's use of the MacGuffin shows he is 'well aware of [his] intention, and that everything [he does] is carefully thought out. And yet, these pictures, hinged around a MacGuffin, are the very ones that some of the critics have in mind when they claim that 'Hitchcock's got nothing to say' (ibid.) But this 'nothing' is actually the way into everything. The MacGuffin is one kind of nothingness in Hitchcock's films which can also been seen as a figure '0', or 'spy hole', like the one Norman Bates (Anthony Perkins) uses to watch Marion Crane (Janet Leigh) disrobe in *Psycho*.

Another case is *North By Northwest*. It is stylish to look at, with glamorous stars, costumes, slick editing and camerawork. Many reviewers at the time took it for nothing more – great entertainment which is, perhaps necessarily, glossy and superficial, a triumph of style over content. On the other hand, however, the film can be seen as quite rich in meaning. This reading can be supported by reference to themes and motifs, visual and spoken. For instance, on one level the 'O' in Roger O. Thornhill (the main character, played by Cary Grant) is the sign of the emptiness at the heart of Thornhill's existence. When asked what the 'O' stands for, Thornhill replies, 'nothing' (reportedly Hitchcock's dig at David O. Selznick's adoption of the middle initial to make himself sound more important). Thornhill's inability to cultivate lasting emotional relationships leaves a hole at the heart of his glamorous and successful existence. On the other hand, the 'O' has another meaning, which is nothing at all, a joke on all those who endow things with deep significance.

Hitchcock's use of sound design also gives a good indication of his creative, and often innovative, approach to cinematic composition, one which frequently emphasises 'nothing' in the form of silence. Some continuity exists between Hitchcock's approach to images based on his early training as a graphic designer and his approach to sound. Hitchcock's attitude to film music was to see it as one among many 'sounds' that could be patterned and structured (*designed*) to produce an effect. He argued, 'when you put music to film, it's really sound, it isn't music *per se*' (Smith, 1991, p. 253). Sound is deployed in innovative ways in several of Hitchcock's films and it often contrasts with, rather than underlines, what is shown visually or what he liked to refer to as the 'pictorial'. Hitchcock was also closely involved in the scoring of his films and gave his composers 'sound notes' relating not only to the use of the music but also to the overall 'sound design' of the scenes (ibid., p. 192).

Hitchcock the technician made sure that he capitalised on the intro- duction of sound as fully as possible. In *Juno and the Paycock* (1929), for example, he wanted to convey 'a medley of noises: the machine guns that were firing down the street; the tinny note of a cheap gramophone playing in the room; the chatter of other people in the room; the tread-tread tramp- tramp of a funeral procession going by' (in Gottlieb, 1997, p. 40). He noted that 'Sound may be used for a stream of consciousness over an unspeaking mouth. It is likewise of great help in expressing the mental processes of the characters' (ibid., p. 221). In *Murder!* (1930), Sir John's (Herbert Marshall) soliloquy in front of his shaving mirror was a technical *tour de force*, with the character's thoughts voiced by the use of a tape recorder and a string orchestra, just out of the camera's view, providing background music. The film is full of playful touches, including a stylised 'call and response' routine in which members of a jury chant rhythmically, 'any answer, any answer, any answer to that Sir John', as the chief protagonist struggles to make sense of the case.

When François Truffaut asked Hitchcock whether he was in favour of university film studies courses the latter replied, 'Only on condition that they teach cinema since the era of Méliès and that the students learn how to make silent films' (in Truffaut, 1965/1986, p. 515). He also said, 'I try to tell my story so much in pictures that if by any chance the sound apparatus broke down in the cinema, the audience would not fret and get restless because the pictorial action would still hold them! Sound is all right in its place, but it is a silent training which counts today' (in Gottlieb, 1997, p. 247). Far from seeing silent cinema as a primitive and flawed prototype for sound cinema, Hitchcock saw it throughout his career as representing the essence of cinema itself, closely related to the concept that he promoted actively throughout his life, 'pure cinema'. However, his idea of pure cinema is often taken mistakenly to mean simply a preoccupation with the pictorial when in fact it is best understood as cinema with minimal dialogue but expressive use of music and sound effects.

Silence occurs in some films for its own sake and sometimes to create the effect of a 'lull before the storm'. In *The Birds*, Hitchcock was particularly satisfied with the sequences based on what he called 'long stretches of almost total silence'. In one of these, he explains, Melanie Daniels (Tippi Hedren) and the Brenner family sit glumly around their sitting room in silence, waiting for the next attack of the birds. Hitchcock drew attention to the lack of dialogue in this scene, noting 'I kept the silence going for quite a bit' (in Smith, 1991, p. 254). Just after this scene there is a noisy, terrifying attack by the birds in which Hitchcock employed electronic bird shrieks to heighten the effect. The contrast between the anxious quiet and the storm of squawking and squealing that marks the arrival of the birds is strikingly effective.

In *Frenzy* (1972) Hitchcock made some of his most devastating use of silence. In one scene, Babs (Anna Massey), a barmaid, emerges out of The Globe pub and into a Covent Garden street. The street is very noisy. Babs walks right up to the static camera until her face fills the screen in an extreme close-up. As she does this, the sounds of the street suddenly vanish for a moment, as if Babs, deep in thought about the identity of the killer, was no longer aware of her surroundings. Suddenly her thoughts are rudely interrupted by the voice of Bob Rusk (Barry Foster), the real killer, as he calls to her. She wheels around in surprise, the noises in the street suddenly returning on the soundtrack as she is jolted back into a reality which is much more terrifying than she realises. The scene changes as the camera follows Rusk and Babs up to his room. We see them go inside whereupon the door is shut. The audience is left to imagine the grisly murder of Babs as the camera makes its way very slowly back down the stairs, through the entrance hall, in complete silence. When the camera gets near the doorway, the sounds of the street filter in. The camera, apparently still in one unbroken take, emerges out into a cacophony of London street sounds (in fact, Hitchcock cuts imperceptibly between a studio set of the house and a location shot of the street, using sound to help conceal the edit). Up above the crowd, the film has shown us a place that is as silent and lifeless as the grave, but out in the streets life goes on in all its rude and bustling chaos. In the first sequence it is Hitchcock's daring use of subjective sound which makes the appearance of Bob Rusk so dramatic. In the second, Hitchcock's restraint puts the audience in a position of having to imagine rape and murder during a silent interlude in the film.

In *Blackmail* (1929), Hitchcock provides another instance of subjective sound. In the scene, Alice White (Anny Ondra), dazed and in terror at having stabbed a man in self defence, cuts herself a piece of bread at the family breakfast table, while a nosy woman stands in the doorway pontificating about the use of a knife as a murder weapon. This is the aural analogue of a point of view shot, with the soundtrack revealing to us what is going on inside Alice's mind, showing how her perception of reality is filtered through her emotions. The annoying visitor persistently refers to knives. But the soundtrack fades on a close-up of Alice's face until only the repeated word 'knife' becomes sharply audible and she is suddenly brought back to reality with a shock, throwing the bread knife aside. A few moments later, the shop doorbell rings and the sound is extended artificially to show how it lingers in Alice's head.

As mentioned in Chapter 1, Hitchcock's films share strong links with nineteenth-century cultural forms. In particular there is the influence of melodramatic theatre, which is relevant to his use of music as well as silence. Melodrama literally means drama with music and although Hitchcock only made a handful of films which might qualify as melodramas from the generic point of view, there are a number of films (including *Lifeboat* (1944) and *Rope*, made without a music soundtrack) which do not use scenes in which the drama is inseparably linked to the use of music. Music and musicians are often at the centre of the drama in the stories, as instanced by the cymbal player in *Man Who Knew Too Much* (1934 and 1956) and by the anti-hero, Manny Ballestrero (Henry Fonda), at the centre of *The Wrong Man* (1957), who is a humble double bass player in a dance band. Another example is the villain in *Young and Innocent* (1937), a drummer in a dance band who gives himself away through his panicked bungling of the song *No One Can Like the Drummer Man*.

Hitchcock's films were conceived from the start as a marriage of music and image, a relationship that he exploited to unrivalled effect in his later films, particularly those made with Bernard Herrmann. Herrmann began his career as a film composer when he was invited by Orson Welles to write the score for *Citizen Kane* (1941). His achievement, in terms of the development of film music, was to have successfully fused the Wagnerian operatic style, which dominated in Hollywood, with the work of modernist composers such as Stravinsky and Bartok. He pioneered

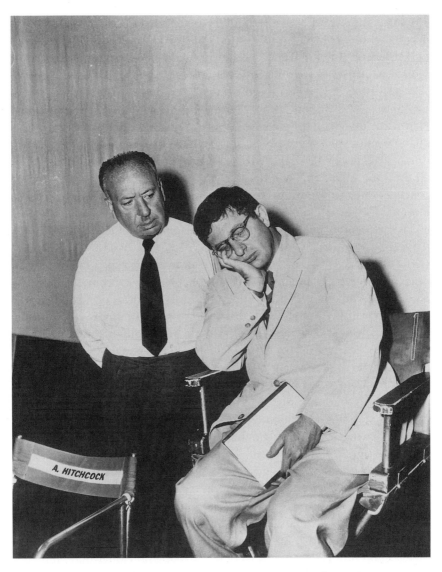

Hitchcock with the composer Bernard Herrmann. Courtesy of Patricia H. O'Connell and Leland H. Faust, Trustees of the Alfred J. Hitchcock Trust.

the use of repetitive motifs, atonality and unorthodox instrumentation (including the use of electronic devices) in Hollywood and his outstanding originality soon came to the attention of Hitchcock. They began their celebrated collaboration on *The Trouble with Harry* (1955), which he conceived as a kind of 'musical portrait' of the director. His subsequent scores for *Vertigo*, *Psycho* and *North by Northwest* won him worldwide acclaim as a film composer.

51

While Hitchcock's story lines often had to conform to Hollywood's demands for happy endings, Herrmann's music emphasised irresolution. As Mark Russell and James Young have observed in *Film Music*, 'the title sequence of *North by Northwest*, for example, ends without resolution, while the conclusion of *Psycho* is accompanied by an unresolved dissonance that can only leave the viewer uncomfortable' (2000, p. 25). Like Hitchcock, Herrmann understood the value of minimalism and restraint. Instead of taking up a golden opportunity for a big musical set piece during the crop duster sequence in *North by Northwest*, Herrmann chose to have no music at all until the final conflagration, thus making his contribution even more effective. One reviewer commenting on *The Wrong Man* wrote, 'The film is a certainty for our 10-best list for 1957 – if for no other reason than that it is a classical demonstration of the uses of extreme quietness in developing suspense' (in Smith, 1991, p. 211).

The film music in *Vertigo* was to feature more strongly than in Hitchcock's other films and his instructions to Herrmann were quite specific, yet he allowed Herrmann artistic licence and trusted his judgement. In the scene where Judy (Kim Novak) emerges transformed into the 'ghost' of the dead Madeleine (Kim Novak), offered up for Scottie's (James Stewart) approval, Hitchcock simply wrote, 'when Judy emerges and we go into the love scene we should let all traffic noises fade, because Mr Herrmann may have something to say here' (in Smith, 1991, p. 220). Herrmann's music provides an instance of meaning that is effectively conveyed although the audience may not be consciously aware of it. Hitchcock himself pointed this out, saying, 'I might argue that I do not want the audience to listen consciously to the music at all. It might be achieving its desired effect without the audience being aware of how that effect was being achieved' (in Gottlieb, 1997, p. 243).

By 1965 the tension between art and commerce which Hitchcock and Herrmann had negotiated so successfully curtailed their relationship when the studio insisted that *Torn Curtain* (1966) should feature a more commercial pop music soundtrack to reflect a changing Hollywood audience. Hitchcock bowed to these commercial pressures, insecure as always about his career, but Herrmann did not adapt so easily. Hitchcock wrote to Herrmann saying:

This audience is very different from the one to which we used to cater; it is young, vigorous and demanding. It is this fact that has been recognised by almost all the European film-makers where they have sought to introduce a beat and a rhythm that is more in tune with the requirements of the aforesaid audience.

(in Smith, 1991, p. 269)

After having convinced the studio he could deliver a pop score which would yield a hit tune, Herrmann set to work on a dark and broody score which Steven C. Smith compares to the one for *Psycho*, calling it 'bizarre' and 'outlandish'. 'Overall', Smith writes, 'Herrmann's music for *Torn Curtain* evokes a steeliness and aridity, an emotional grey versus the black-and-white contrasts of *Psycho* or the colourful romanticism of *Vertigo*.' Hitchcock's response was swift and brutal: 'I heard the first segment and I said "Finished, no other way, finished; goodbye, here's your money, sorry"' (ibid., p. 272). The score which was eventually used for the film was provided by a young British composer, John Addison. It too failed to yield a hit tune.

In addition to his use of silence and orchestral scores, Hitchcock also employed skilful use of what might be called 'ambient sound', that is sound appearing to emanate from the environment in which the story is set. When analysing film soundtracks a distinction can be drawn between what is called *diegetic* and *non-diegetic* sound. Diegetic sound has its source in the world of the film, for example music coming from a radio or hi-fi that one of the characters is listening to. Non-diegetic sound is heard 'over' the world of the film and is most often in the form of an orchestral score, composed specially for the film. Very often, Hitchcock uses diegetic sound in preference to non-diegetic sound. In *Rope*, for instance, there is orchestral music over the beginning and end credits but for the rest of the film Hitchcock restricts himself to sound sources, such as the piano in the drawing room, that come from within the world of the film.

One scene in particular stands out in this respect. Brandon (John Dall) and Philip (Farley Granger), two young men who live together in a smart New York apartment, have murdered a fellow student, David Kentley (Dick Hogan), for kicks. Brandon has organised a dinner party, the centre point of which will be the chest in which they have hidden the body. Philip, however, lacks the nerve to keep up the façade and begins to exhibit increasingly neurotic behaviour, alerting the suspicions of his former prep school master, Rupert (James Stewart), who questions him closely as he sits and plays the piano. The piece being played is the first part of Poulenc's *Movements Perpetuele*, which is marked by the use of occasional and disquieting dissonances. Philip plays to try to calm himself but the dissonances keep creeping into the music, as Rupert gets closer to the truth. Meanwhile, Rupert plays with the metronome, stopping and starting it, increasing the tension and suspense until Philip begins to crack up. The piano music and the rhythm of the metronome are used as a counterpoint to the dialogue. A more ironic use of counterpoint occurs shortly afterwards as Mrs Wilson (Edith Evanson), the housekeeper, busies herself with tidying the dinner things off the chest in which the body has been hidden.

The camera stays on her as she innocently goes about her business while the soundtrack is of the guests anxiously discussing the whereabouts of David.

For *Rear Window* (1954), Hitchcock had initially rejected the idea of a music soundtrack because there were so many sounds that he wanted to come from within the film itself. In the end he hired Franz Waxman to provide a musical score in order to realise his idea that the narrative should be paralleled by the efforts of the composer in the film to finish writing a song. Hitchcock told Bogdanovich that 'at the start you would hear one finger on the piano banging this song out trying to get it, and then improvising on it as the picture went along, getting two hands going, and then eventually at the climax of the film, he puts a record on and there's a whole new song' (in Bogdanovich, 1997, p. 523). The resolution of the musical puzzles and obstacles confronted by the composer (Ross Bagdasarian) accompanies the resolution of the mystery element of the film.

Rear Window also features a complex web of sounds coming from radios, stereos and street sounds, which often provide poignant commentary on the action. At one point, the song *Mona Lisa* is heard wafting through the night air, from a radio or hi-fi in the apartment building opposite. Lisa is the name of the central character played by Grace Kelly. While the song is playing we see Miss Lonelyheart (Judith Evelyn) in the apartment opposite fend off the unwanted sexual advances of a man she has invited over for a romantic dinner. After she has thrown him out she contemplates suicide. The song is unusually resonant on number of levels, mainly through its suggestion that the perception of a loved one as a romantic object might be ambivalent and deceptive: 'Are you warm and real Mona Lisa, or just a cold and lonely, lovely work of art?' It can be taken to refer to the romantic problems of both Miss Lonelyheart and the hero, Jeff (James Stewart), in reconciling their images of an ideal with reality.

Hitchcock also used abstract electronic music with *The Birds*, which featured avant-garde, electronically generated squawks and shrieks from Remi Gassman and Oskar Sala, reflecting the current high-culture vogue for *musique concrete*. Hitchcock's approach here was expressionistic in terms of his use of sound and he admitted that 'the sound of birds wings and birds cries will be stylised to some extent' (in Cameron and Perkins, 1963, p. 4). Evidently, however, he didn't see the soundtrack for *The Birds* as departing so much from his conception of what film music is and does.

Elizabeth Weis (1985) has argued that Hitchcock draws parallels between the bird sounds and the sounds associated with Melanie Daniels (Tippi Hedren) earlier in the film. In particular, she notes how her drive down to Bodega Bay is accompanied only by the amplified sound of her sports car engine, with occasional screeches from the tyres as she hurtles along the road. 'It may be', she suggests, 'that Hitchcock wants us to identify Melanie with mechanical noises because at this point we are to perceive her behaviour as cold and mechanical' (Weis, 1985, p. 309).

Once Melanie has arrived, the peace of the little hamlet is contrasted with rude interruptions from her car engine's noise. The disruptive nature of her presence later prompts a woman to accuse her of having brought the bird attacks with her. Soon after her arrival she makes a trip across the bay with only the sound of her motor boat's engine on the soundtrack, once again associating her with mechanical, unnatural sound. Hitchcock himself has discussed the way in which he used the screech of a truck engine to convey the pain of Mitch's mother (Jessica Tandy), just after she discovers the mutilated body of Dan Fawcett, saying, 'The screech of the truck engine starting off conveys her anguish. We were really experimenting there by taking real sounds and stylising them so that we derived more drama from them than we normally would.' Hitchcock endows material objects with animal qualities here, speaking of an 'emotional truck. . . . It's as though the truck were shrieking' (in Truffaut, 1965/1986, p. 224).

Through his manipulation of sound and silence, then, Hitchcock fashions compelling and often jarring relationships between what the audience sees and what it hears. Sometimes underlining, sometimes counterpointing, but always enhancing the overall effect of the film on the audience, sound acts as an inseparable aid to the effectiveness of the image. As Hitchcock himself pointed out, sound 'is in its own way . . . an image maker' (in Gottlieb, 1997, p. 221).

4 Realism and *The Wrong Man*

The extent to which Hitchcock designed his films might suggest that they are contrived and unrealistic. From the start of his career, Hitchcock was criticised for the lack of realism in his films. *The Bioscope*, reviewing *The Mountain Eagle* in 1925, complained that 'in spite of skilful and at times brilliant direction, the story has an air of unreality' (in LaValley, 1972, p. 49). André Bazin classified him as a director who believed in 'the image' rather than reality (1968, p. 26). Hitchcock himself claimed that 'I put first and foremost cinematic style before content. . . . I don't care what the film is about . . . content is quite secondary to me' (in Gottlieb, 1997, p. 292). But formalism and realism can be seen as complementary rather than opposed tendencies. Close attention to his work shows that Hitchcock's formalism and his interest in realism are not only compatible but also constantly in a creative tension. He outlined his philosophy in an article written for the journal *Cine-Technician* in 1948:

> *I don't try to put onto the screen what is called 'a slice of life' because people can get all the slices of life they want out on the pavement in front of the cinemas and they don't have to pay for them. On the other hand, total fantasy is no good either – I'm speaking only for myself remember – because people want to connect themselves with what they see on the screen. The story . . . must be believable, and yet not ordinary. It must be dramatic, and yet lifelike. Drama, someone once said, is life with the dull spots removed.*
> *(Gottlieb, 1997, p. 205)*

He also famously claimed in an article published in *The Sunday Times* on 6 March 1977, that what he aimed to give his audience was not a slice of life, but a piece of cake.

Part of the difficulty in appreciating the realism in Hitchcock's work is that he identified himself strongly with melodrama, which tends to be seen as sensationalist rather than realistic. While directing *Waltzes From Vienna*

(1934), Hitchcock told actor Esmond Knight, 'I hate this sort of stuff, melodrama is the only thing I can do' and, as we have seen, the influence of nineteenth-century melodramatic theatre remained with Hitchcock throughout his career. Hitchcock points out that the term 'melodrama' has largely pejorative connotations and that it suggests 'behaviour which is hysterical and exaggerated'. However, 'unvarnished realism' would strike the audience as unreal, because of what he calls the 'habit of drama' in the minds of the audience. This predisposition 'causes the audience to prefer on the screen things that are outside their own, real life experience'. There arises the problem, then, of 'how to combine colour, action, naturalism, the semblance of reality, and situations which will be intriguingly unfamiliar to most of the audience'. He concludes that his own 'greatest desire is for realism. Therefore I employ what is called melodrama – but which might as well be called ultra-realism – for all my thinking has led me to the conclusion that there is the only road to screen realism that will still be called entertainment' (Hitchcock, 1936, pp. 1–2).

Until the 1960s, melodrama had been associated with lowbrow entertainment and realism with high art. Booth writes that 'melodrama has been treated with general contempt by dramatic historians and critics. The adjective melodramatic is today derisively applied to anything vaguely considered unnatural or exaggerated; sometimes it seems to be used as a synonym for old' (Booth, 1964, p. 9). Hitchcock's films tended to suffer from the bias shown by critics towards realism and against melodrama. Criticisms of *The Man Who Knew Too Much* (1956) in American periodicals such as *Nation* and the *New Yorker* turned on the issue of realism where it was unfavourably compared to the 1934 version (Kapsis, 1992, pp. 42–3). In general, Hitchcock's American films were judged inferior to his English ones for their lack of realism by British critics, such as Lindsay Anderson, who wrote approvingly of *Blackmail* (1929) that '[t]he everyday locales – a Corner-House restaurant, the police station, the little tobacconist's shop where the heroine lives with her parents, empty London streets at dawn – are authentic; the characters are believable'. However, the American films were 'committed to all that is worst in Hollywood – to size for its own sake . . . to the star system for its own sake, to glossy photography, high-toned settings, lushly hypnotic music scores' (in LaValley, 1972, p. 54).

Hitchcock, by contrast, emphasised his ambition, even in fantasy, 'to be as life-like as one can'. He argued that his suspense films were 'nightmares for an audience' and that dreams themselves had a kind of clarity and definition which he was trying to capture: 'When you have a nightmare it's awfully vivid' (in Gottlieb, 1997, p. 313). Cathartic pleasure felt by an audience, he maintained, is facilitated by a combination of absorption and distance. In a 1949 article for *Good Housekeeping* he argued that 'the suburban matron whose eyes all but pop out of her head with excitement as she watches the cinematic blade approach the cinematic neck would no doubt faint dead away if she encountered a similar problem in her home. Why, then, does she enjoy it in the movies?' (ibid., p. 117). His answer was that it represented a 'double bind' for the spectator in which the audience knows very well at a rational level that it's just a movie but nevertheless, maintains another level of belief in contradiction to this, which is able to invest emotionally in the drama as if it were real. 'Fear and fear not', he explained, 'that is the essence of melodrama. Fear the saw may dismember the ingénue. Fear not: it won't' (ibid., p. 118). In order to achieve this effect it is necessary for the audience to perceive a high degree of correspondence between what is shown on the screen and what is familiar to them from their everyday experience.

Hitchcock's films show a keen interest in documenting everyday activity. This kind of sociological imagination was much in vogue in Britain during the 1920s and 1930s. In *The Ring* (1927), for instance, there are extended sequences in the film which contribute little or nothing to the progress of the narrative but instead convey images of the sporting sub-culture of boxing in 1920s London, moving between the fair ground and the Albert Hall, all the time noting details concerning behaviour and milieu. The opening of *Rich and Strange* (1931) is a wordless three minute sequence, in which we are shown hordes of office workers leaving their offices, opening their umbrellas in the rain, and piling on to the London Underground. The opening shot is a long single take with the camera opening on a clerk's ledger, then zooming out to take in the whole office with rows and rows of clerks leaving their desks. The camera then pans across to the locker area, where a group of bowler-hatted men jostle with each other to get out, then further across to the corridor where the women workers are surging forward to get out of the building in a hurry. Then the camera cuts to the exterior of the building where crowds of office workers put up their umbrellas in synchronisation with each other. On the Underground, the rush hour crowds push and shove each other, causing the protagonist, Fred Hill (Henry Kendall) to pull the feather from a woman's hat, while opposite a young man tucks into a ham sandwich with indecent relish. Although comic, the scene is also realistic, with the camera being used to register these many small details and rituals of everyday life. The sequence is reminiscent of the opening of *Blackmail*, with its documentary depiction of routine police work.

In addition to their eye for detail, ritual and everyday routine, many of Hitchcock's films show an awareness of contemporary events within the real world. A good example would be the siege in *The Man Who Knew Too Much* (1934). In the film, a group of anarchists hide out in a house besieged by the police who engage in a shooting match with them. Hitchcock ran into difficulties with the censor over the scene as it recalled a real-life event, the Sydney Street siege, which Hitchcock remembered from his childhood. Here, a group of anarchists were tracked down by unarmed policemen who called in the army. The censor was unhappy about the police being shown armed and, in a compromise settlement, Hitchcock agreed to show guns arriving on a lorry and being handed out to police. In that scene, Hitchcock took care to provide the detail of a policeman being handed a cup of tea in the middle of the shootout. 'I did this because I have always found that in a moment of crisis a person invariably does something trivial, like making a cup of tea or lighting up a cigarette' (in Gottlieb, 1997, p. 199).

The set designer for *Vertigo* (1957), Henry Bumstead, went to great lengths to research how the characters might have lived in real life. Bumstead and Hitchcock went to visit the apartment of retired police graduates with college degrees in order to get Scottie (James Stewart)'s apartment looking authentic. Bumstead made Scottie a philatelist, and put stamp magazines and a magnifying glass in a corner of his living room. 'That's the kind of detail Hitchcock loved to see', he explained (in Ettedgui, 1999, p. 20). Such detail is important not to the story but the establishment of character and milieu as authentic. As Hallam and Marshment put it, '[t]heir purpose is to persuade us that this is the kind of environment which these people would inhabit if they were real people, that these kinds of people would inhabit this environment in real life' (2000, p. 81).

It must be remembered that realism in cinema relies not so much on fidelity to life as on an effect of 'verisimilitude' (plausibility) which is partly achieved through the accumulation of details which are often superfluous to the story itself. All fiction aims, in varying degree, to create the illusion of reality or the effect of reality through the use of tried and tested techniques. Whether the audience accepts a fiction as plausible depends to a large extent on what Roland Barthes called 'doxa', that is public opinion (Barthes, 1977). Mainstream film-making operates on the basis of a mutual understanding between the film-makers and the audience about what the audience will accept as plausible; this, in turn, is related to the conventions of particular genres, such as musical, horror movie, women's picture, etc. Through time, the public consensus will change, often leaving old films looking very unrealistic. But also over time, film artists have experimented by mixing genres in unexpected ways.

In a discussion on film realism, Stephen Prince (2001) suggests that the public are curious about the relationship of film to reality and find added interest in the knowledge that a film is based or partly based in actuality. He also suggests that audiences enter into a 'contractual' understanding with the film-maker concerning what they are about to see. The terms of this contract may be adjusted by the film-maker prior to the viewing of the film by the audience. Hitchcock put a great deal of thought into negotiating his contracts with the audience. There was a general contract, discussed by Kapsis (1992), which Hitchcock established himself over the course of his career. This contract specified the director as a maker of thrilling and sensational fictions which nevertheless featured ordinary people in ordinary locations. Hitchcock's contract with his audience generally offered (but did not always guarantee) certain specific pleasures such as thrills, spills and laughter. But there were also contracts for particular films which he would often try to negotiate through his personal addresses to the audience. One was for *Psycho* (1960), where he specified that his audience must not arrive late for the film or reveal its ending. Another was for his trailer *Marnie* (1964), a film which has a notoriously problematic relation to realism owing to its sometimes absurdly stylised look. Hitchcock attempted to address the issue of genre by highlighting it as a film which is 'very difficult to classify' but which could perhaps be described as a 'sex mystery'. The text which follows his speech asks, 'is Alfred Hitchcock's *Marnie* . . . a sex story . . . a mystery . . . a detective story . . . a romance . . . a story of a thief . . . a love story? . . . YES AND MORE!' The audience, not knowing quite what to expect, were confused and disappointed by the film. Unfortunately for Hitchcock, expressionism was not recognised as a generic category by his audience, otherwise he could perhaps have accounted for the flamboyant liberties which he took with realism by categorising it for his audience as an expressionist sex mystery.

The conventions of the form known as naturalism also enabled a contract in which the audience might accept the co-existence of melodramatic and realist tendencies in Hitchcock's films. In 1868, Emile Zola's *Thérèse Raquin*, a key work of naturalism, was attacked for its implication that 'horror and madness' were integral to 'the drama of modern life' (Zola, 1868/1962, p. 26). *Psycho*, with its exploration of horror and madness in the midst of everyday life and its love of sordid, realistic detail, is a direct descendent of this brand of naturalism. A reviewer in *Time* was disgusted by 'one of the messiest, most nauseating murders ever filmed. At close range, the camera watches every twitch, gurgle, convulsion and haemorrhage in the process by which a living human becomes a corpse' (in Rebello, 1990, p. 165).

However, perhaps the most striking instance of Hitchcock addressing the expectations of his audience directly is to be found in *The Wrong Man* (1957) where Hitchcock appeared at the beginning of the film itself to explain to the audience its foundation in fact:

> *This is Alfred Hitchcock speaking. In the past I have given you many kinds of suspense pictures, but this time I would like you to see a different one. This*

difference lies in the fact that this is a true story – every word of it. And yet it contains elements that are stranger than all the fiction that has gone into many of the thrillers that I've done before.

Here Hitchcock challenges the common-sense response of his audience who might be inclined to dismiss the story with its outlandish co-incidences, as too far-fetched, even for fiction.

Given the explicitly negotiated contract with the audience in respect of *The Wrong Man*, it is worth considering more closely. Hitchcock made the film for Warner Brothers as a favour to the ailing company for no salary. It has similarities with other Warner Brothers 'social problem' films, such as *I Am a Fugitive from a Chain Gang* (1932), which also dealt with the ordeal undergone by a wrongfully accused man. Warner's films frequently aimed for naturalism and, as in *The Wrong Man*, attempted to copy the shooting style of newsreels (as in *The Public Enemy*, 1931). The film was also made at a time when new lightweight camera equipment made shooting on location, rather than in the studio, much easier and more fashionable. *The Wrong Man* has been seen as one of Hitchcock's most and least typical films. Rohmer and Chabrol described it as a film which 'brings together the themes scattered throughout his work' (1992, p. 145). The film refers back to *I Confess* (1951), in its theme of a holy innocent whose self-belief is tested to the limit on being wrongly accused of a crime. It also refers forward to *Vertigo*, *Psycho* and *Marnie* with its stress on madness. However, its semi-documentary visual style and lack of humour made the film seem atypical to Hitchcock audiences.

The Wrong Man is the most self-consciously realist of all Hitchcock's films. Inspired by the true story of Manny Balestrero (Henry Fonda), who was wrongly accused of robbery, the film involved a labour of elaborate reconstruction in order to get as close as possible to actuality. Hitchcock told Truffaut that 'everything was minutely reconstructed with the people who were actually involved in that drama. . . . We shot on the locations where the events really took place. Inside the prison we observed how the inmates handled their bedding and their clothes. . . . We also used the actual psychiatric rest home to which the wife was sent and had the actual doctors playing themselves' (Truffaut, 1965/1986, p. 358). Members of the Balestrero family were also on set to ensure the authenticity of the film (Krohn, 2000, p. 180).

Furthermore, Hitchcock went to some lengths to evoke realism by abandoning the high-gloss surface finish which had characterised his previous American films such as *To Catch a Thief* (1954) and *The Man Who Knew Too Much* (1956). He hired cinematographer Robert Burks to shoot the film, warning him: 'Perhaps you may not want to do this picture, Bob.

I wouldn't want the stark, colourless documentary treatment I expect to reflect on your reputation as a photographer' (Deutelbaum, 1986, p. 214). Hitchcock had 'emphasised that he wanted it shot like a newsreel shot' (ibid.).

However, as Sterritt has pointed out, 'Hitchcock changed the actual events of the Balestrero case in many ways, treating it not as an inviolable set of facts, but rather as a vehicle for exploring themes that interested him' (Sterritt, 1993, p. 78). Although based on a true story, *The Wrong Man* has strong literary and mythical associations with the biblical story of Job (for the drawn-out sufferings of its hero which test his faith), Kafka's novel *The Trial* (1925) (for its account of an ordinary man who endures a living nightmare of bureaucratic humiliation) and *Bleak House* (1853) by Charles Dickens (for the interminable miscarriage of justice suffered by humble folk). Hitchcock changed certain details, as Deutelbaum notes: 'The weak points of the police investigation, the ease with which Balestrero was able to establish his alibis, and the effectiveness of his attorney have been eliminated from the screenplay' (Deutelbaum, 1986, p. 209). On closer examination it appears that Hitchcock was less interested in strict fidelity to the facts and was more concerned with the 'the play of fact and fiction' (ibid., p. 212).

To start with, Hitchcock's cameo at the beginning of the film gives an ironic twist to his claims of realism because the opening is so highly stylised. He appears in extreme long shot, in silhouette, casting a long shadow on a vast deserted and artificially darkened studio lot. His appearance sets the visual tone for the film which revels in the play of light and shadow. The film features a great many exaggerated high and low angle shots, particularly during scenes when Manny is in police custody. The opening image of the Stork Club is a location shot, but is filmed slanted, from the left. There is extensive use of cross-hatched shadows, particularly those cast across Manny's cell. These elements are expressionistic in the extreme, as is the shot of Manny in jail, closing his eyes in despair as the camera revolves, causing the cell to spin on screen. The presence of these expressionistic elements has led to the film's frequent categorisation as a *film noir* (for example, Hirsch, 1981; Silver and Ward, 1980) However, the elements which really give the film its *noir* character have more to do with the co-presence of expressionism and seedy naturalism. For instance, in the room where Manny is questioned by the police, a large, messy hole can be seen in the wall, indicating that the police station (and, by implication, the justice system) is in an advanced state of disrepair. The apartment block, visited by the Balestreros in an attempt to find an alibi for Manny is similarly decrepit. This 'warts and all' realism in tandem with the attempt to depict faithfully how reality looks subjectively, through the eyes of a character who is under considerable emotional duress, is exemplary of *film noir*. The film is also *noir* by virtue of its depiction of the city and city life as integral to the story. One poster for the film proclaimed: 'Warner Brothers present Henry Fonda and Vera Miles and the exciting city of New York in Hitchcock's *The Wrong Man*', thus exemplifying the critical commonplace that in *film noir* the city is like a leading character (Christopher, 1997).

It is also possible to see in the film's realism an indictment of the false promises of the emerging consumer society of the 1950s in America, a *noir*-ish ideological stance in itself. If this is the case, then the film can be read, by extension, as one intimately concerned with the relationship between the romance of consumerism and the reality of debt. Near the beginning of the film, on a subway ride home, Manny reads a newspaper in which there is an advertisement for a Ford car, promising family fun (an ironic touch, given the devastation which is shortly to be wreaked on Manny's own family). The coincidence of the ad for the car with an ad for 'The New York Savings Bank' also reminds us that we are in the midst of a very specific historical moment: 1950s American consumer society where dreams of owning new status symbols go hand in hand with the social realities of debt brought on by the need to borrow more than is earned. The impetus to borrow, of course, comes from the desire to keep up with the expectations of living standards generated by advertisements.

This scene closely parallels another in *Rich and Strange*. Like Manny, Fred Hill is on his way home from his routine job on an Underground train when he starts to look at advertisements promising a better life. He looks up at the ads on the wall of the train and sees one for fashion clothing ('Clothe Your Wife at Garridges') and another for a fancy restaurant called the Majestic. Fred opens his newspaper at a third which asks 'Are you satisfied with your present circumstances?' Both Manny and Fred lead humdrum lives and dream of bettering themselves through consumer goods. As a result of an ordeal, both of them rediscover the value of human relationships.

There, however, the similarities end. Manny's home life is relatively contented (unlike Fred's bickering relationship with his wife) and his flaw, if it can be so-called, is not so much greed as a kind of unthinking conformism to the imperatives of bourgeois family life. As Sterritt sees it, 'Hitchcock does not seek to demolish his characters or their way of life in the name of cultural criticism. What he does seek to demolish is complacency, here manifested in the assumption that middle-class values and middle-class virtues and behaviours will bring fulfilment and contentment in their wake. . . . Manny and Rose have done everything "right". Yet they are dogged by uncertainty and decay' (Sterritt, 1993, p. 71).

The Wrong Man has been described as 'one of the bleakest films in the history of cinema' (Silver and Ward, 1980, p. 319). Why then did Hitchcock feel the need to make such an uncharacteristically serious and sombre film? Two reasons suggest themselves: first, he owed Warner Brothers a film under a previous contract and the film has many of the characteristics of a Warner Brothers social problem film with its emphasis on the underside of city life and the injustice meted out to the poor. Secondly, he cannot fail to have been aware of the kudos that Italian neo-realist cinema had been gathering in America. Films by Rosselini, De Sica and Fellini had been gaining a sizeable audience in America. As Robert Ray notes, 'the discovery that there was an audience sizeable enough to make even these bleak movies profitable unsettled the American film industry' (in Kapsis, 1992, p. 49). Hitchcock even tried to get Cesare Zavattini, who had worked with Antonioni, Fellini and De Sica and who had written the script for *Bicycle Thieves* (1948), to work for him in 1965 on an idea that would become *Torn Curtain* (1966) (De Rosa, 2001b, p. 1). Furthermore, Manny Balestrero, as played by Henry Fonda, is very similar to the lead character Antonio Ricci (Lamberto Maggiorani) in *Bicycle Thieves*, being tall, gaunt, down at heel and sad-eyed.

The film turned out to be a box-office failure. However, its failure was not altogether inevitable and may have been due to the inability of the marketing department at Warners to understand the ways in which the Hollywood audience was starting to fragment: 'The likely market for *The Wrong Man* should have been the more educated film-goer who after the war had discovered the European art film. Before the 1950s, the American film industry had viewed its potential market as a more or less undifferentiated mass' (Kapsis, 1992, p. 48). The irony was that there was an art house audience, attuned to a more European, realist aesthetic, who might well have been more receptive to the film had it not come with Hitchcock's name attached to it.

Truffaut put the failure of the film down to its direction. He told Hitchcock, 'You're trying to make the public identify with Fonda, but when he goes into his cell, for instance, you show the walls spinning in front of the camera. That's an antirealistic effect. I feel it would have been a good deal more convincing if you had simply shown Henry Fonda sitting on a stool in the cell.' Hitchcock replied, 'Maybe so, but wouldn't that be rather dull?' To which Truffaut countered that the film 'should have been done in a very objective way, with the camera always at normal level, like a documentary; it should have been handled like a newsreel reportage.' Hitchcock's final word on the matter makes clear that he has no intention of compromising his role as a commercial film-maker in the interests of higher aesthetics or morality: 'It seems to me', he tells Truffaut, 'that you want me to work for the art houses' (Truffaut, 1965/1986, p. 366).

Hitchcock, as ever, clearly had his mainstream audience in view when he fashioned the optimistic ending of the film. However, his intentions have been misconstrued. Donald Spoto has written that 'The film's final shot (of a family strolling in a tropical setting) and on-screen words (that Rose was released two years later completely cured and the family lived happily ever after) were added by the studio, over Hitchcock's loud objections' (Spoto, 1976, p. 257). Similarly, Sterritt writes that 'the last shot is pure *noir*, countering an unhappy narrative and ambivalent plot resolution with a tacked on happy ending that couldn't be more deliberately unconvincing' (Sterritt, 1993, p. 69). Recent research by Steven de Rosa has uncovered correspondence between Hitchcock and his writers Angus MacPhail and Maxwell Anderson 'which reveals that Hitchcock fully intended both the final shot of the Balestrero family in Florida as well as the epilogue'. MacPhail wrote that Hitchcock 'would like the film to end on a note of warm reassurance and not a chilling reminder' (in De Rosa, 2001a, p. 2). Here again it is worth stressing that Hitchcock's commercial sensibility prevailed over any purist concern for the 'unvarnished' truth.

The Wrong Man does, however, continue a thematic preoccupation with truth which runs through much of Hitchcock's work. The film can be seen as truly Hitchockian for its suggestion that perception and truth are not always co-extensive. Perception may be coloured by less than noble motives. The women who work in the insurance office, motivated by paranoia and an impulse to conform, back each other up in their wrongful accusations until everyone seems to believe in Manny's guilt. Even Rose begins to doubt him. However, the outcome of the film seems to endorse La Bruyere's caution in *Les Characteres* that 'sometimes the truth is the exact opposite of what is generally believed'. In this respect, the film might be compared to an episode of the *Alfred Hitchcock Hour, I Saw the Whole Thing*, in which a novelist (John Forsythe) defends himself in court against a charge of careless driving. A string of witnesses come forward, swearing that they saw him skip a red light, causing the death of motorcyclist. The novelist gently probes each witness for their motivation in making the accusation. He establishes that private bitterness, resentment and the desire to back up the official story have caused each witness to imagine mistakenly that they saw the crash clearly. Eventually the writer wins his case, establishing the culpability of the motorcyclist. The final blow to the reliability of these witnesses turns out to be that he had not even been in the car at the time of the accident; he had been covering up for the real driver, his pregnant wife.

The view of the world presented in *I Saw the Whole Thing* and *The Wrong Man*, as in so many other Hitchcock dramas, is located at the crossroads between seeing, feeling, truth and illusion. As Maurice Yacowar puts it: 'Hitchcock's basic interest has always been in how our perceptions reshape the world. His realism constantly shades off into the expressionistic imagery and extravagant technical devices by which he conveys the realism of the emotional state' (Yacowar, 1986, p. 21). That the films should take up this theme is in the end so much more interesting than the question of whether they are adequate to some strictly empirical notion of 'reality'. Hitchcock's sophisticated approach to representation has not always been adequately appreciated and his films have often been seen as personal testimony or confession. However, a more nuanced and complex view of the relationship between cinema and reality can be of particular help in relation to one of the most vexed of all issues in Hitchcock scholarship, the relationship between the man, his films and women.

5 Hitchcock and women

In 1935 Barbara J. Buchanan wrote of 'Hitch's brutal disregard for glamour, love-interest, sex-appeal and all the other feminine attributes which the American director considers indispensable' (in Gottlieb, 1997, p. 79). Hitchcock had clearly gained a reputation as a misogynist, for as early as 1939 an interviewer, J. Danvers Williams, confronts him with it, going on to remark that he is well known 'for treating his women characters unsympathetically' (ibid., p. 92). But the representation of women in his films, especially in the 1940s and 1950s, is complex and shot through with contradictions.

At first sight, the charge of conscious misogyny seems to fit at least some of the available evidence. For instance, Hitchcock quoted the advice of the nineteenth-century dramatist Victorien Sardou, whose formula for successful drama was 'torture the women' (in Spoto, 1983, p. 458). Hitchcock's screenwriter, Evan Hunter, was horrified at the director's idea for the rape scene in *Marnie* (1964): 'Evan,' Hitchcock is reported to have said, 'when he sticks it in her, I want that camera right on her *face*' (in Hunter, 1997, p. 76). Writing of *Strangers on a Train* (1950), the critic David Thomson argued, 'Miriam, Guy's wife, is a viper, egging on her own death, and just one example of the Hitchcock films' tight-lipped fear and loathing of women' (Thomson, 1979, p. 28). James McLaughlin catalogues some of the fates which befall Hitchcock's heroines: 'Alicia is punched in the face and poisoned; Miriam is strangled; Judy is dragged to the top of a church bell tower, off which she falls and dies; Marion is stabbed to death; Melanie is attacked by birds and pecked until she's unconscious (Annie Hayward is pecked until she's dead); Marnie is tormented psychologically; and Brenda is strangled; Charlie is gassed, tripped down a flight of stairs, and almost thrown in front of a speeding train' (McLaughlin, 1986, p. 147).

Mothers in Hitchcock films such as *Notorious* (1946), *Psycho* (1960), *The Birds* (1963) and *Marnie* are particularly problematic characters. In *Notorious*, for instance, Mme Sabastian (Leopoldine Konstantin), is a monstrous black widow, who comes up with the idea of slowly poisoning Alicia (Ingrid Bergman) to death. It is she, not her Nazi son, Alexander (Claude Rains), who provides the embodiment of unambiguous evil. When Peter Bogdanovich points this out Hitchcock responds: 'Well, I suppose, generally speaking, Mother can be a bloody nuisance. . . . Sometimes she can be all-pervading. She can hang around and interfere with everybody's life' (Bogdanovich, 1997, pp. 537–8).

Many critics (for example, Cohen, 1995; Corber, 1993; Jancovich, 1996; Spoto, 1976) have remarked on the significance of *Psycho*'s monstrous mother in relation to popular fears about 'momism' – a term which had come to prominence through a best-selling book by Philip Wylie, *A Generation of Vipers* (1946). Wylie had argued that the ideal of motherhood in American society bred women who suffocated their sons by pampering them. In consequence, a generation of American men were growing up emasculated, dependent and conformist. Although Wylie's book was published in 1946, fears of momism intensified in the 1950s with the growth of a new suburban ideal, in which 'mom' was given the leading role. The character of Mrs Bates stands as one of the most extreme representations of such fears. The psychiatrist's summing up at the end of the film strongly reinforces the suggestion that she is responsible for Norman's condition, having been 'a clinging and demanding woman'.

While mothers were monstrous or neurotic, other kinds of women in Hitchcock's films seemed idealised. The films are famous for their blonde actresses whose coolness and composure is shattered by a horrifying experience. Hitchcock made his preference for the 'cool blonde' type well known and from as early as *The Lodger* (1926), this figure has been a central prop in his films, often linked with a fetishistic desire on the part of the male protagonist. In *The Lodger*, one of the first shots we see is of a sign promising 'tonight, golden curls'. Subsequently the audience learns that a serial killer has been murdering girls selected on the basis of their hair type and colour. The Polish actress Anny Ondra, who appeared in *The Manxman* (1929) and *Blackmail* (1929), was an early prototype of Hitchcock's own fascination with blonde-haired women. Hitchcock was open about his tastes, linking his preference for reserved actresses with a cool exterior to the concept of suspense and telling Truffaut: 'You know why I favour sophisticated blondes in my films? We're after the drawing room type, the real ladies who become whores once they're in the bedroom' (in Truffaut, 1965/1986, p. 337).

After the filming of *The Birds* (1963), Hitchcock's reputation as a woman hater, not just in art but this time in life, received a further boost when Tippi Hedren reported that she had been subjected to a cruel ordeal during shooting. Hitchcock had taken a week to film the scene in which she is attacked by birds in an attic; instead of the artificial birds that she had been promised, he had used real birds, thrown at her by the prop hands. She finally collapsed after one of the birds drew blood on her face. This frequently recounted story appeared to confirm that the director was a cruel misogynist who, in his increased frustration that these cool blondes took no interest in him sexually, had turned from torturing the heroine on screen to tormenting her off screen too.

This view of Hitchcock was reinforced by critical studies of his work. In 1973, Molly Haskell published her landmark feminist history of women in Hollywood film, *From Reverence to Rape*. In it she refers to Hitchcock's 'feeling for the similarity between sexual and homicidal impulses' and argues that a long line of blondes in Hitchcock films, including Madeleine Carroll in *The 39 Steps* (1935), Grace Kelly in *Rear Window* (1954), Eva Marie Saint in *North By Northwest* (1959), Janet Leigh in *Psycho*, Tippi Hedren in *The Birds* and Barbara Leigh-Hunt in *Frenzy* (1972), show that the fair-haired woman is 'reprehensible not because of what she does, but because of what she withholds: love, sex, trust'. She argues that they must be punished by 'long trips through terror' (Haskell, 1973, p. 349). Haskell contrasts the blonde characters with the brunettes, like Kim Novak as Judy in *Vertigo* (1957), Diane Baker in *Marnie* and Suzanne Pleshette in *The Birds*, whom she sees as '"good", that is down to earth, unaffected, adoring, willing to swallow her pride' (ibid., p. 349). However, she argues, Hitchcock is not attracted by this type, he wants the type who is most likely to reject him and so 'the misogynist in Hitchcock invests the character with poisonous personality traits to punish her for rejecting him. She is exquisitely beautiful, but frigid, snooty, uncaring' (ibid., p. 350).

Adhering to this view of Hitchcock's misogyny, Spoto's *The Dark Side of Genius* (1983) tried to show that the director was a cruel and bitter man who took pleasure in inflicting pain on women. Spoto acknowledges the greatness of the films but he depicts Hitchcock as a man of dwarfish moral stature. But, as even Spoto acknowledges, the paradoxes and contradictions involved here are considerable and complex. First, Hitchcock appeared to get on particularly well with the women in his own life, much better, in fact, than with his male acquaintances. He trusted women with some of the most important aspects of his work and gave them considerable responsi- bilities. He discussed all the important decisions concerning his films with his wife, Alma, and he trusted her judgement better than his own. He happily admitted that 'I rely on her opinion . . . she tries to be on set the first day we begin shooting, sometimes goes to rushes and always gives me her criticisms. They're invariably sound' (in Gottlieb, 1997, p. 53). Joan Harrison was employed as a much-valued scriptwriter and later producer of his TV show. His other chief confidants were his personal secretary,

Suzanne Gauthier, and his personal assistant, Peggy Robertson. Karen Black, who appeared in *Family Plot* (1976) remarked that 'whoever said he is a misogynist is a very silly, mistaken person. . . . I think he liked women. And I think that you can communicate best about that which you have an affinity for. And I think he had an affinity for women, and that's why they came across so well' (in Garrett, 1999, p. 81).

Furthermore, Hitchcock claimed that his films were aimed primarily at the women in the audience. He argued that this was for commercial reasons and criticised British film-makers for not paying more attention to the female audience. He told André Bazin that 'Hollywood films are made for women; it is toward their sentimental taste that scenarios are directed because it is they who account for the bulk of the box office receipts. In England films are still made for men, but that is also why so many studios close down' (Bazin, 1972, p. 65). The emphasis on women's films in Hollywood during the 1940s was heavily influenced by the fact that so many men had been drafted into the army to fight and the industry perceived that women comprised a majority of the audience (Waldman, 1983, p. 30). The films produced by David Selznick, *Rebecca* (1940), *Spellbound* (1945) and *The Paradine Case* (1948), centre on their strong women characters. *Rebecca* in particular, with its use of female voiceover and subjective point of view camerawork, exemplifies the Hollywood women's picture of the 1940s. Raymond Durgnat has suggested that 'the influence of Selznick had sensitised [Hitchcock] to themes and settings which enabled him to combine suspense with a middle-class women's angle' (1974, p. 19). Durgnat also classifies *Psycho* as a woman's film, a slightly eccentric judgement perhaps, but not altogether implausible given the centrality of Marion Crane to the first half of the narrative which bears insistently and sympathetically on her point of view. The opening of the film is concerned with relationships and feelings, rather than action, which is a typical feature of the Hollywood woman's film. Furthermore, it is Marion's sister Lila (Janet Leigh) who is the real investigator.

When Truffaut complains about the 'icy sexuality' of Grace Kelly in *To Catch a Thief* (1954), saying, 'my guess is that this is one aspect of your pictures that's probably more satisfying to the feminine viewers than to the male audience', Hitchcock's response is to point out that it is usually the woman who chooses which film to go and see and that 'it's generally the woman who will decide later on whether it's been a good picture or a bad picture' (Truffaut, 1965/1986, p. 337). It is important to stress that Hitchcock set out to make films that he thought that women in the audience would find compelling and enjoyable. Furthermore, in recent years, it is feminist critics who have tended to take centre stage in arguing about whether Hitchcock's films are 'good' or not.

Joan Fontaine as the title character in *Rebecca* (1940), Hitchcock's first fully fledged woman's film. The producer David O. Selznick encouraged Hitchcock to take an interest in 'feminine things'. © ABC Photography Archives.

Molly Haskell's pioneering feminist study was followed by a wave of feminist criticism, much of which was highly theoretical in its orientation and often more ambivalent in its conclusions. Laura Mulvey's essay 'Visual Pleasure and Narrative Cinema', first published in 1975, was not specifically about Hitchcock's films but it used *Vertigo* and *Rear Window* as examples of the ways in which the cinema has been used as an apparatus to shore up male narcissism and to offer women limited possibilities for identification. Drawing on psychoanalytic theory, she argued that the processes involved in gaining pleasure from mainstream cinema were unconscious and that the film-maker followed the rules of conventional narrative which were motivated by latent male fears and desires concerning women. In a now famous passage, Mulvey wrote: 'In a world ordered by sexual imbalance, pleasure in looking has been split between active/male and passive/female. The determining male gaze projects its fantasy onto the female figure which is styled accordingly' (1975, p. 11).

For Mulvey there seemed to be little room for a woman's subjectivity, as a character in a film or as a spectator, that was not first organised around her objectification by men. She drew attention to the predominance of voyeurism and fetishism in films such as *Rear Window* and *Vertigo*, arguing that these two modes of representation provided a means through which to control and contain the threat that female sexuality represented to men's social dominance. Mulvey argued that 'scopic drives' were unconscious and used another psychoanalytic term, scopophilia, to describe the compulsive character of cinematic voyeurism. However, Hitchcock's exploration of voyeurism and fetishism was, to a significant degree, conscious, as Mulvey perhaps acknowledges when she writes, 'he takes fascination with an image through scopophilic eroticism as the subject of the film' (1975, p. 15). In a discussion of James Stewart's role in *Vertigo*, Hitchcock told Bogdanovich that 'We play on his fetish in creating this dead woman, and he is so obsessed with the pride he has in making her over' (Bogdanovich, 1997, p. 529).

Similarly, when Truffaut asks Hitchcock what made him want to adapt the book on which *Marnie* is based he says:

The fetish idea. A man wants to go to bed with a thief because she is
a thief, just like other men have a yen for a Chinese or coloured woman.
Unfortunately, this concept doesn't come across on the screen. It's not as
effective as Vertigo, *where Jimmy Stewart's feeling for Kim Novak was*
clearly a fetishist love.

(*Truffaut, 1986, p. 464*)

In contrast to Mulvey's account, however, Hitchcock attributes the fetishistic impulse to his female characters too, explaining Grace Kelly's interest in Cary Grant in *To Catch a Thief* as based on her fetishistic interest in his criminal past. Mulvey's account draws heavily on Freud's theories and it is interesting to note that Freud did not accept that women could experience fetishistic desire (a view strenuously challenged by Gamman and Makinen (1992)).

Tippi Hedren as the title character in *Marnie* (1964). Courtesy of Universal Studios Licensing LLLP.

With regard to voyeurism, once again Hitchcock was consciously explor-ing, rather than unknowingly indulging in, its problematic nature, in films such as *Rear Window*. Mulvey's influential reading of the voyeurism in films such as *Rear Window* and *Vertigo* is that *it has associations with sadism: pleasure lies in ascertaining guilt (immediately associated with castration), asserting control and subjecting the guilty person through punishment or forgiveness. The sadistic side fits in well with narrative. Sadism demands a story, depends on making something happen, forcing a change in the other person, a battle of will and strength, victory/defeat.*

(Mulvey, 1975, p. 14)

Such a description certainly seems to fit *Vertigo* quite well. However, she assumes that the active spectator of the feature film is male and that the organisation of looks within the film privileges the male leading character.

Is this so in Hitchcock's films? With regard to *Notorious*, for instance, there is a striking use of mise-en-scène in the second scene where the camera is positioned behind Devlin's (Cary Grant) chair during a party given by Alicia Huberman (Ingrid Bergman). Devlin can only be seen in silhouette and his character has not yet been introduced to the audience. However, Alicia directs most of her attention at him in the scene. He appears as a mysterious, shadowy, yet all-important presence. Renov (1980) interprets the placement of the camera as an indication of Grant's dominance, made to stand for the imperialistic gaze of the male spectator in the audience (and by extension, within society). Yet close examination of the film would suggest that this is not the only possible reading of the scene. Although placed behind Devlin's chair, the camera moves towards him and slowly over to one side putting him in on one side of the frame, half out of the picture. Its movements do not seem co-extensive with Devlin's own field of vision. It would make more sense to say that the camera treats him as viewed object, rather than as all-powerful viewing subject. In the course of the story, Devlin is revealed as something of a sadist and a man in need of a lesson about his relationships with women. From the outset the film is taking a critical distance on his character which enables the audience to see him as Alicia will come to see him: a dark, bullying figure, whose attempts to control women are motivated by weakness rather than strength.

It is all too easy to conflate Hitchcock the real-life person with the persona implied by his films. However, this would be far too simplistic and fails to take account of the degree to which his public persona was highly constructed both positively and negatively in a series of media stereotypes. In particular, the ironic distance in his film-making is easily overlooked. As the director himself insisted, 'I have no identification with my characters. If I did, I couldn't picture them as objectively as I do' (in Bogdanovich, 1997, p. 527). It has long been accepted in narrative theory that the critic must be attentive to the differences between real author, implied author and narrator (see, for example, Cobley, 2002). It is certainly interesting to speculate, as Modleski (1988) does, that Hitchcock *unconsciously* oscillated between objectification and identification. But Hitchcock himself gave several indications that he was quite conscious of his tendency to cross-identify with men and women. He said of the infamous extended kiss in *Notorious* that the audience were given 'the great privilege of embracing Cary Grant and Ingrid Bergman at the same time'. In this connection, Charles Bennett's comment that 'there's no part in any picture he made, woman or man, that Hitchcock couldn't have played himself' is resonant (in Bouzereau, 1993, p. 183). Hitchcock's feminine identification is also echoed in the comment, made by his wife Alma, that, 'When I gave birth to our only child, Pat, I had a relatively easy time of it, but Hitch suffered such panic pains, he might as well have changed places with me' (ibid., p. 182). All of this fits well with Freud's (1979) account human sexuality as inherently bisexual, with repressed elements of sexuality emerging as aspects of role-play in fantasy but it does not require a psychoanalytic theory of the unconscious to explain it. Hence there are two dangers here: the first is to read the films as wilful personal confessions of Hitchcock's darker wishes; the second is to deny agency to the film-maker and to see him determined by unconscious drives. Both perspectives are likely to produce reductive accounts of the films.

In *Vertigo*, Donald Spoto argues that Scottie (James Stewart) is a surrogate for Hitchcock himself. Judy/Madeleine (Kim Novak) is shown as a woman who is manipulated and controlled for Scottie's sexual pleasure. As Scottie says to Judy towards the end of the film, commenting on her earlier relationship with Gavin Elster (Tom Helmore), 'He made you over just like I made you over. . . . Did he train you? Did he rehearse you? Did he tell you what to do and what to say?' The assumption that Scottie functions as a mouthpiece for Hitchcock's own desires and frustrations is seductive in its simplicity but highly problematic in its failure to take account of the problem of *representation*, the complex and highly mediated process by which links are inferred between image and actuality. The error is to imagine that representations are *directly* expressive of anything or anyone. The representations of Scottie's desires might bear some relation to Hitchcock's own feelings but the only thing we can be sure of is that this will be a highly abstracted, partial and probably distorted image. To neglect this point is to collapse the real author (Hitchcock), the implied author (Spoto's interpretation of Hitchcock based on his reading of the films) and narrator (Scottie) into one.

To be fair to Spoto, his own analysis isn't so simplistic and does bring into play the idea that perhaps Hitchcock identifies with both Stewart and Novak, exploring both male and female aspects of his psyche, but this reading still runs the risk of confusing the real author with the fictional characters on questionable evidence. Certainly, though, it is important to point out that the film is more than just Scottie's story. At first sight, the film appears to be obsessively centred on Scottie's point of view. Hitchcock sticks to him so closely that for the first half of the film the camera does nothing but watch him or show us what he sees through numerous point of view shots and sequences. However, at a crucial point in the story, Scottie is absent and the camera focuses intently on the character of Judy Barton. She relates in a flashback, the story of how she came to be the victim of a plan to deceive Scottie by pretending to be Gavin Elster's wife, Madeleine. Elster has murdered his wife and used Judy to impersonate her in an elaborate plot to convince Scottie that he has witnessed Madeleine's suicide. Up until this point, Kim Novak's profile has been the dominant image of her. However, as she presents her story in flashback Hitchcock has her turn full face into the camera, to look directly at the audience. According to some versions of film theory, such moments break the illusion created by the film and return the audience to a more critical reality. However, Durgnat has argued that direct address to the audience of this kind is a well-established convention in mainstream films and tends 'to occur at moments of character sincerity' (Durgnat, 2002, p. 54). If so, Judy's confession gains in its heartfelt quality and solicits the empathy of the audience through the use of the device.

The film turns around this scene. Until now, the sympathy of the audience has been engaged for Scottie, culminating in his humiliation at the inquest on Madeleine's death. Through Judy's flashback, the true story of Madeleine is revealed and the riddle of Judy's uncanny likeness to her is solved. But more than that, the scene accomplishes Judy's entry into the narrative as a subject rather than an object. For the first time in the film, the audience has access to her thoughts and feelings, most importantly her confession that she is in love with Scottie and desperately wants him to love her for 'what she is', rather than for her resemblance to the fantasy figure of Madeleine that she helped to create to in order to fool him. In subsequent scenes we see the couple together in various locations (at Ernie's restaurant, walking along the picturesque San Francisco streets side by side, dancing at a supper club) that ought to be romantic for both of them but which are instead frustrating and disturbing for Judy, as we see from the shots of her anxious face throughout. The purpose of these scenes is to build up sympathy for Judy, in preparation for the ordeal which she is about to undergo in the next set of scenes where Scottie becomes monstrous in his attempts to transform her into the object of his fantasy. From the flashback scene onwards, the film will centre on shots of Judy and Scottie as a couple, filmed mostly in shot-reverse shot (cutting backwards and forwards between Judy and Scottie) or two shot (Judy and Scottie in the same frame together). The language of the film has transformed from the insistent focus on Scottie in the first half, in which he is the centre of attention and sympathy, to a focus on the relationship between Judy and Scottie, in which Scottie has become an aggressor. Furthermore, it is Judy's suffering and longing which is at the emotional heart of the film from now on. The information provided by Judy in the flashback provides the suspense for the final act of the film. From there on, the audience will be anxious for her safety and her state of mind – will Scottie find out that she lied to him and is an accomplice to the murder of Elster's wife? Will her longing for Scottie to love her for herself find fulfilment? These are the enigmas at the centre of the film's focus on the personal lives of Judy and Scottie.

However, reading the film through the optic of gender on its own is apt to miss out on the multilayered concerns of the story. If we follow the film more closely, it emerges that it is as much about class as it is about gender, a point which Spoto seems to overlook. Madeleine is an old world, European, aristocratic figure. She is contrasted first with the modern American, 1950s ideal of classlessness of Midge (Barbara bel Geddes), who remains unimpressed by the aristocratic aura of Madeleine's portrait. However, it is the contrast between Madeleine's aristocratic style and Judy's lower-class identity which is one of the chief driving motors of the narrative. What Judy lacks is old money class. Scottie tries to buy it for her. Quite clearly, Scottie is obsessed not by Madeleine as a person (he doesn't even hear her speak before he becomes entranced by her), but as an image of aristocratic sophistication and power. One could say he is the subject of this power. As with Manny in *The Wrong Man* (1957), Hitchcock has cast a tall, lanky actor to play a 'little man' in the social hierarchy. Scottie's social subordination is made graphically clear in the early scene where he meets Gavin Elster, an old acquaintance and former equal, who has risen to the upper classes through his marriage to Madeleine. Throughout the meeting, the mise-en-scène emphasises Elster's social superiority through the framing of the shots and the design of the set (which is constructed on two levels) and is used to position Elster as the bearer of power and authority.

The scene in Elster's imposing office connects to the theme of class and money politics to sexual politics and to history. The same phrase, concerning the 'freedom' and 'power' of men is repeated three times during the film. The first time the words are uttered is in the imposing office of Gavin Elster. Indicating a map of San Francisco in 1845, Elster professes nostalgia for the days when there was 'colour, excitement, power, freedom'. Elster is a shipping magnate and the 1840s were the heyday of men who made fortunes in rail, shipping and other heavy industries. However, what is merely implicit in this scene (the domineering machismo of Elster, who

Judy and Madeleine in *Vertigo* (1957), both played by Kim Novak. The contrast between Madeleine's aristocratic style and Judy's lower class identity is one of the chief driving motors of the narrative. Courtesy of Universal Studios Licensing LLLP.

sees his power and freedom under threat), is made explicit when Scottie and Midge visit a local historian, Pop Lebel (Konstantin Shayne), to find out more about Carlotta Valdez, Madeleine's great grandmother. Pop Lebel tells how Carlotta was driven mad by her husband, 'a rich and powerful man', who got her pregnant, then took her child and abandoned her. 'A man could do that in those days', Lebel explains, 'they had the power and the freedom'. Finally, at the climax of *Vertigo*, Scottie will complete the circle by invoking the words for the third and final time when he finds out that he has been deceived by Elster and Judy. 'With all of his wife's money, and all that freedom and power, he ditched you', Scottie taunts Judy. During this speech Scottie links himself to Elster ('he made you over just like I made you over'), who now emerges as his dark double. Envying the potency of Elster, Scottie has tried to imitate his mastery over women and failed. Scottie's impotence, dramatised so blatantly in his fear of heights, has been ironically counterpointed throughout the film by a series of phallic objects. In case this sounds far fetched, we have Hitchcock's own instruction to set designer Henry Bumstead that San Francisco's Coit Tower must be visible from Scottie's apartment for the sole reason that 'it's a phallic symbol' (Ettedgui, 1999, p. 14). (The cranes visible from Elster's office also function as exaggerated symbols of his masculine potency.)

The film is often described as Hitchcock's most personal, which in naïvely instrumental readings might suggest that it is the guilt-ridden confession of how he desired to manipulate his actresses. In 1997 Greg Garrett confronted a group of women who had acted in Hitchcock films with Spoto's argument that *Vertigo* is a thinly disguised account of the director's obsession with controlling women. Karen Black quickly rebuffs the suggestion saying, 'He's not that controlling. There's a lot of people who write books about him who have never been in the room with him'. Black's defence of Hitchcock is then endorsed by Janet Leigh (although Tippi Hedren remains silent) (in Garrett, 1999, p. 83). Perhaps these women are the victims of false consciousness but then again, perhaps it's the critics who have got it wrong. Certainly, by focusing entirely on Hitchcock's supposed persona, Spoto's well-known analysis has the effect of obscuring a whole culture of bad behaviour towards women in Hollywood. Kim Novak has claimed that she was attracted to the role of Judy/Madeleine because it told the truth about the treatment of women in Hollywood. During the filming of *Vertigo* it is reported that producer Harry Cohn kept Novak constantly watched, forced her to stay in her dressing room eating only food prepared under his orders, and called her 'the fat Polack' (Wexman, 1986, p. 35).

It might be true to say that in portraying men's cruelty towards women, Hitchcock's films offer the audience at least two axes for identification, one identifying with the male aggressor, the other with the female victim. Hitchcock himself may well have had something invested in both positions (then again he might not). Robert Samuels (1998), commenting on this duality, refers to the films as 'bi-textual', while Robin Wood (1989) and Tania Modleski (1988) have argued that through this cross-gendered identification, Hitchcock's films reveal something of the dynamics of a patriarchal society. Modleski argues 'neither that Hitchcock is utterly misogynist nor that he is largely sympathetic to women and their plight in patriarchy, but that his work reveals a thoroughgoing ambivalence about femininity' (1988, p. 3). The view that Hitchcock's films reveal an oscillation between identification with and objectification of women has found widespread acceptance among critics. It functions as a sophisticated response to the problematic representation of women in Hitchcock's films and fits the evidence best. It enables a better understanding of Hitchcock's position as an 'unmanly man' (sedentary, neurotic and artistic) in a patriarchal society, the performance of his actors, and the internal dynamics of camera placement and editing – so perhaps it is worth considering, even if it does not (and should not) provide definitive closure on the 'woman question' in Hitchcock's films. On this count at least, Hitchcock's admonition to Ingrid Bergman that 'it's only a movie' conceals a great deal.

6 Delirium of interpretation? The uses and abuses of psychoanalysis

A great deal of commentary, much of it feminist in orientation, has been written on Hitchcock's films from a psychoanalytic perspective and several of Hitchcock's films refer to psychoanalysis. To what extent can it be said that Hitchcock's films are Freudian and how appropriate is it to apply psychoanalytic theories to the interpretation of them? During the 1980s and 1990s the use of psychoanalytic theories became a dominant tendency in film studies, especially in the case of Hitchcock's films. As Raymond Durgnat observes in his study of *Psycho* (1960), psychoanalysis is a 'theory of first resort' (2002, p. 4). The work of Mulvey (1975) and Modleski (1988), discussed in the previous chapter, makes use of psychoanalytic theory and their work is only part of an extensive catalogue of studies which draws on Freudian and Lacanian ideas. Yet as far back as 1974, Durgnat had warned against what he called 'the delirium of interpretation', that is the over-interpretation of Hitchcock's films, particularly under the influence of Freudian theory.

It might sometimes appear that the volume of scholarly work which has applied psychoanalytic theory to Hitchcock has saddled the films with extraneous or irrelevant theoretical baggage. There are significant book-length studies of the films by Wood (1989), Bellour (2000), Žižek and others (1992) and Samuels (1998) and numerous articles where the approach is avowedly psychoanalytic. Other critics such as Barr (1999) and Sterritt (1993) employ the terminology of psychoanalysis (especially the Oedipus complex) on an *ad hoc* basis to interpret the films. The resort to psychoanalysis in order to explain Hitchcock's films has been widespread but controversial. However, psychoanalytic theories were certainly known to Hitchcock and several of his films, including *Spellbound* (1945), *The Wrong Man* (1957), *Psycho* and *Marnie* (1964) feature psychoanalysts as characters. Freud's name also crops up frequently in the films. In the shooting script for *The Lady Vanishes* (1938), a joke is made out of the way Iris (Margaret Lockwood) mistakes Miss Froy's (Dame May Whitty) name for Freud; later in *Marnie*, the eponymous heroine (Tippi Hedren) says ironically, 'You Freud, Me Jane' to Mark Rutland (Sean Connery). In *Spellbound*, Hitchcock even has actor Michael Chekov, playing eccentric psychoanalyst Doctor Brulov, made up to look like any caricatured Middle European psychoanalyst but, especially, Freud.

There are also two explicit references to psychoanalysis in *Rope* (1948). In the first, Janet Walker (Joan Chandler), a young woman guest at a dinner party given by Philip (Farley Granger) and Brandon (John Dall), is quizzing Philip (who, unbeknown to her, has just strangled her fiancé) about why he doesn't eat chicken. He replies, with some irritation and nervousness, that there is no reason, to which Janet responds, 'there must be a reason – Freud says there's a reason for everything'. Later on in the same film, Rupert Cadell (James Stewart), the boys' former teacher, returns to their apartment to catch out the murderers under the pretence of retrieving a cigarette case. 'Completely unlike me to forget it, isn't it', he tells them. 'I suppose a psychoanalyst would say that I didn't really forget it at all. I unconsciously left it because I wanted to come back. But why should I want to come back?'

In *Rear Window* (1954), Stella (Thelma Ritter), a nurse, comments on the state of modern relationships, berating the influence of psychoanalysis: 'Modern marriage. . . . Once it was see somebody, get excited, get married. Now it's read a lot of books, fence with a lot of four-syllable words, psychoanalyse each other until you can't tell the difference between a petting party and a civil service exam', and in *Frenzy* (1972), two lawyers (Gerald Sim and Noel Johnson) analyse the psychology of the serial killer using Freud's concept of the 'pleasure principle'.

Much of the psychoanalysis in Hitchcock's films might be dismissed as mere 'pop-Freud' – an oversimplified, populist rendering of complex ideas designed to tie in with contemporary publicity which often sensationalised Freud's work. However, a good deal of the emphasis on psychoanalysis came from Hitchcock's writers, and in the case of Ben Hecht (*Spellbound*, *Notorious*, 1946) and Joseph Stefano (*Psycho*) he seems to have selected them partly on the basis of their somewhat deeper interest in Freudian themes. The script for *Spellbound* was checked and supervised by the prominent psychotherapist May Romm, who at that time was treating the film's producer David Selznick and his wife Irene using Freudian methods (Freedman, 1999). The Surrealist artist Salvador Dali, whose ideas inspired the French psychoanalyst Jacques Lacan, was engaged to create dream imagery for the film. Aware that many people in the audience would not be familiar with the theory of psychoanalysis, Selznick insisted on some text accompanying the opening credits to explain psychoanalysis to the audience, which ran:

In *Notorious* (1946) Alex Sebastian (Claude Rains)'s perverse relationship with his mother (Leopoldine Konstantine) and his wife (Ingrid Bergman) has strongly Freudian overtones. © ABC Photography Archives.

This movie deals with psychoanalysis, the method by which modern science treats the emotional problems of the sane. The psychoanalyst seeks only to induce the patient to talk about his hidden problems, to open the hidden doors of his mind. Once the complexes that have been disturbing the patient are uncovered and interpreted, the illness and confusion disappear . . . and the evils of unreason are driven from the human soul.

Although Hitchcock was not consistent or expert in his use of psycho-analytic motifs, he was hardly innocent of Freud's work and even without the intervention of his script writers, psychoanalytic ideas inform other films of his in less direct form. Patricia Highsmith's novel, *Strangers on a Train* (1950/1999), for example, provided him with a psycho-sexual drama, the homosexual elements of which, however, he toned down considerably in his film version, mainly for the censor's benefit. Highsmith writes of Bruno: 'He longed for Guy to be with him now. He would clasp Guy's hand, and to hell with the rest of the world', suggesting that he is homosexual (Highsmith, 1950/1999, p. 151). But in the novel, unlike the film, Guy becomes obsessed with Bruno to the extent that, in a repressed frenzy, he murders Bruno's father for him. Even then, Highsmith introduces a strong element of ambiguity, such that it is unclear whether they are in love (knowledge of which is repressed by Guy) or whether they should be read as two facets of human nature, symbolically represented by the two characters: '[H]e and Bruno. Each was what the other had not chosen to be, the cast off self, what he thought he hated but perhaps in reality loved' (ibid., p. 163). The book reveals a strongly Freudian understanding of sexuality and identification in which Bruno exists partly as a projection of Guy's secret desires.

This emphasis is carried over into the film version, in which, as Wood suggests, it is as though Bruno understands Guy better than he understands himself. This is because, 'he is an extension, an embodiment, of desires already existing in Guy' (1989, pp. 87–8). In psychoanalytic terms, Bruno functions in the story partly as what Freud might have called a *projection* of Guy's unconscious wishes – to be violently rid of his tiresome ex-wife, Miriam. Furthermore, the romantic attachments which Guy professes towards Ann Morton (a senator's daughter, played by Ruth Roman) are unconvincing to Bruno, who suggests that her attraction lies in her social status rather than any personal qualities. The suspicion that noble protestations conceal baser unconscious motives is also a characteristically Freudian one. A further psychoanalytic reference point is provided in Bruno's relationship with his parents, which is stereotypically Oedipal: he flirts with his mother and has a murderous hatred of his father, whom he plots to kill.

The Oedipus theme is present in numerous places in Hitchcock's work. The centrality of Freud's Oedipus theory to *Psycho* is a result of input from two sources. The first is the novel *Psycho* by Robert Bloch, who explains 'in the late fifties Freudian theories were very popular and . . . I decided to develop the story along Freudian lines. The big Freudian concept was the Oedipus fixation, so I thought, "Let's say he had a thing about his mother"' (in Rebello, 1990, p. 9). The second influence comes from the screenwriter Joseph Stefano, who was in analysis at the time the film was in preparation. Stefano remarked that during the discussions of the script with the director, 'we were getting into Freudian stuff and Hitchcock dug that kind of thing' (ibid., p. 47). The references to psychoanalysis in the story were present in Norman's pointedly Oedipal references to his relationship with his mother (including the lines 'a boy's best friend is his mother' and, more ironically, 'A son is a poor substitute for a lover'), which were picked up by the censors who tried unsuccessfully to get the offending lines excised.

Towards the end of the film, a psychiatrist explains how Norman took on his mother's identity after he had killed her in a fit of Oedipal jealousy once she had taken on a new lover. The closing images of the film are of Marion's car being dredged up from the swamp. Hitchcock disagreed with Bogdanovich's literal-minded suggestion that it had been necessary to show this sequence at the end in order to establish that the money had been recovered. Hitchcock's explanation is more Freudian: 'It was in a sense a material manifestation of what had emerged through the psychiatrist's explanation' (Bogdanovich, 1997, p. 533).

Hitchcock worked in a cultural climate where Freud's theories were widely disseminated and found to be of interest. It had become something of a commonplace for Hollywood films of the 1940s and 1950s to feature psychiatrists and psychoanalytic ideas. Hollywood had taken to psychoanalysis early on with Samuel Goldwyn offering Freud, 'the greatest love specialist in the world' $100,000 to advise on 'a really great love story' in 1925 (in Lebeau, 2001, p. 34). Freud's ideas were known to American audiences, especially in the 1940s and 1950s, through the extensive media coverage which they received, often in connection with soldiers returning from the Second World War, who were treated for shock using Freudian methods.

However, it can be argued that the most convincing case for reading Hitchcock's films alongside psychoanalytic theory lies in the numerous points at which their more general worldviews seem to converge. Allen (2000) points out that Hitchcock grew up in an era which had a fascination about perversion and criminality. Several notable figures came up with psychological theories which proved influential. First, there was the novel *Dr Jeckyll and Mr Hyde* (1886) by Robert Louis Stevenson, in which a respectable doctor invents a potion which turns him into a murderous sex maniac. Stevenson provided a coda to the story in which Dr Jeckyll seeks to explain his transformation in terms of a hidden dark side present in all men. Later, the German sexologist Krafft-Ebbing coined the term 'lust murder' to describe the sexual pleasure which murder produced in some individuals.

The best example of this in Hitchcock's work would be Bob Rusk's (Barry Foster) chanting of the word 'lovely' as he rapes and strangles Brenda Blaney (Barbara Leigh Hunt), the owner of a dating agency, in *Frenzy*, although there are numerous other examples such as Bruno's (Robert Walker) satisfied smile as he strangles Miriam (Laura Elliott) in *Strangers on a Train*. Truffaut (1965/1986) points out the importance of this link when he remarks that in Hitchcock's films the love scenes are filmed like murders and the murder scenes like love scenes. However, it is Freud's contribution to the debate about the psychology of sex and perversion that had the greatest impact in Hitchcock's own time and on his films. It was Freud's influence that led to a blurring of the boundaries between the normal and the perverse, since he had suggested that normality is a kind of a front or concealment for darker and more perverse desires. In 'Civilisation and Its

Discontents' (1991), Freud had written that civilised living is only possible through the forcible repression of our darkest and most shameful wishes, which can erupt in the course of everyday life. According to psychoanalysis, aggressively controlling, murderous and incestuous wishes intrude into the most orderly and respectable lives. Robin Wood has observed of Hitchcock's films that 'ordered life depends upon the rigorous and un-natural suppression of a powerfully seductive underworld of desire'. He refers to this view as the 'essence of Hitchcock' (Wood, 1989, p. 94).

Furthermore, Hitchcock, in common with Freud (and the nineteenth-century German philosopher Arthur Schopenhauer), had an interest in exploring the ways in which events, people and things are distorted, misrepresented or are deliberately overlooked through subjective per-ception. As with Freud's (1991) theory of the pleasure principle and the reality principle, Hitchcock's films posit the objective existence of a real world (the acknowledgement of which is generally healthy) in contrast to subjective distortions of it (which are often shown as harmful to others, for example, in *Vertigo* (1958), Scottie's failure to see Judy for herself). Denial of reality has become one of the most resonant themes of psychoanalysis. As Dr Brulov puts it in *Spellbound*: 'The human being doesn't want to know the truth about itself.'

Freud's comedy of middle-class manners and misrecognition, *The Psycho-pathology of Everyday Life* (2002), finds an analogue in Hitchcock's parade of complacent bourgeois characters forever getting it wrong. Often characters with glasses in the films see what they want to see, fail to see, or blindly agree with what others say they have seen. Characters wearing glasses frequently mislead or confuse other characters. The bespectacled recep-tionists in *The Wrong Man* and in *Frenzy*, confidently (and vindictively) mis-identify criminals. In *Spellbound*, Dr Brulov (Michael Chekhov), the 'brilliant' and apparently perceptive psychologist wrongly insists on the guilt of John Ballantine (Gregory Peck), a man accused of murder who has lost his memory. The lawyer in *Young and Innocent* (1937), who wears comically thick spectacles, is incompetent. Some of these figures, such as lawyers, doctors and academics, belong to recognisable stock characters in popular entertainment and are there for the audience to ridicule, espe-cially when they dispense useless, misleading and confusing advice. There is, for instance, the ornithologist in *The Birds* (1963), who pompously assures everyone that birds are quite incapable of turning on human beings, moments before a devastating attack. But others are ordinary folk themselves, complacently blind to the truth of the world around them. Mrs Wilson (Edith Evanson), the housekeeper in *Rope*, busies herself with tidying up after a dinner party, wearing her thick glasses. As the guests discuss the whereabouts of David Kentley (Dick Hogan) in front of her,

Mrs Wilson daintily dusts down the chest in which his body has been hidden. While other characters in the film become wary and suspicious, she takes little notice of the world around her, ignoring all the clues to the murder and burying her head in her housework.

The influence of Expressionism and Surrealism, both of which drew on psychoanalysis, led to Hitchcock's interest in the way in which the world appears to someone in an intense emotional state or with a fetishistic investment in things. In *Notorious*, Alicia's (Ingrid Bergman) vision is repeatedly distorted. When driving with Dev (Cary Grant) her hair falls in front of her eyes obscuring the road in front of her as she proceeds in a drunken state; she also sees a distorted and upside down Dev when she wakes up from the resultant hangover. The moral of such episodes of misrecognition is that people see what they desire to see. In the process they cause, perpetuate or become accomplices in harm done to others and to themselves. This is a critical perspective which Hitchcock's films sometimes extend beyond the world of the film and towards the cinema audience itself, perhaps implicating the audience in the crimes they avidly watch.

Another area of overlap is that Freud and Hitchcock shared a fondness for the short stories of E.T.A. Hoffmann, who explored the horrors associated with doubles and split personalities. Freud wrote a famous essay on Hoffmann's *The Sandman*, called 'The Uncanny' (1985), in which he argued that the disturbing strangeness of such stories is actually the result of their being all too familiar reminders of our innermost repressed fears and desires. Freud made great play around the associations of the German word *unheimlich*, which he explains has connotations of both the strange and the familiar. It is also connected with the German word for home (*Heim* – whereas *heimlich* means secret). The idea of bringing strange and disturbing things into the realm of the homely is behind much of Hitchcock's working method. The brutal and botched murder of a man in a kitchen using first a kitchen knife, then a spade and finally a domestic gas oven in *Torn Curtain* (1966) for instance, gives the terror a concrete and familiar anchor in the world of ordinary domesticity.

The family home is frequently the site of fear, anxiety, betrayal, madness and even murder. Hitchcock used the home as an instance of the everyday that he was so keen to get on screen and once said of television that one of its 'greatest contributions is that it brought murder back into the home where it belongs' (Gottlieb, 1997, p. 58). In *The Lodger* (1926) and *Shadow of a Doubt* (1943), young women live under the same roof as men who fall under suspicion of being serial killers. *Rebecca* (1940) and *Suspicion* (1941) play on the anxieties of newly married women. Mrs Verloc (Sylvia Sydney) in *Sabotage* (1936), stabs her husband with a carving knife over dinner after discovering that her young brother has been blown up by a bomb given to him to carry by her husband, who is in the pay of terrorists. Alicia Huberman (Ingrid Bergman) is poisoned and kept prisoner in her bedroom in *Notorious*. In *The Wrong Man* an ordinary family home is devastated when the husband is wrongly accused of murder and the wife goes mad as a result of the strain. Such scenarios had become a staple of the Victorian sensation fiction which Hitchcock grew up reading. One commentator has written of the finest of these stories, *The Woman in White* (1860) by Wilkie Collins, that 'home is a place where you fall ill, and risk being murdered or driven insane' and the 'secret theatre of home', a phrase coined by Collins himself (Sweet, 1999, p. xiv), would be apt to describe many of the scenes in Hitchcock's films, such as the moment in *Sabotage* when Verloc is suddenly stabbed by his timid wife driven to desperation, using the knife she has just used to prepare the family meal.

What is disturbing is already within the home but unacknowledged as such. The arrival of a sinister figure at the family home has been fore-shadowed by the revelation of some murderous desires lurking there. In *Shadow of a Doubt*, Joe (Henry Travers), a slightly eccentric patriarch, com-petes with his friend Herb (Hume Cronyn) to devise a foolproof murder plan by which one might dispatch the other without being caught. Their playful and ineffectual game, based on their fascination with crime literat-ure, is given ironic force when Joe's brother-in-law, Uncle Charlie (Joseph Cotton), arrives and subsequently turns out to be a serial killer. Uncle Charlie's niece, also called Charlie (Teresa Wright), has a relationship with her uncle which is bordering on the incestuous – he gives her a ring as a present and calls her 'my girl'. Young Charlie and Uncle Charlie are linked in numerous ways throughout the film. When we first see young Charlie, she is lying on her bed in the same pose as her uncle at the start of the film. Young Charlie tells her uncle that they are 'like twins'. Finally, Uncle Charlie brings out a murderous side to his niece when she tells him to leave the family home or 'I'll kill you myself'. Without making any direct reference to Freud or psychoanalysis, *Shadow of a Doubt* exemplifies the Freudian theme that murder and perverse sexuality lie not outside bourgeois family and the civilised community but barely under the surface of it. As Uncle Charlie says, 'the world is a foul sty. Do you know that if you ripped the fronts off houses you'd find swine?'

In *The Lodger*, a serial killer, known only as the Avenger, has been terrorising London. He is known to have a preference for 'golden hair'. Immediately before the arrival of the Lodger (Ivor Novello), who is subsequently suspected of the killings, Hitchcock, with characteristic edgy playfulness, shows us a young couple, Daisy (June Tripp) and Joe (Malcolm Keen), discussing the day's news in the kitchen of their home, where Joe is making dough. 'I'm keen on golden hair myself, just as the Avenger is', Joe tells her as he cuts determinedly into the dough with a pastry cutter to make a love heart. Evidently, Daisy is less keen on Joe, for she tears the love heart in half and throws it back at him. In one short and apparently light-hearted domestic exchange, Hitchcock has given us simple but potent images which connect Joe with sexual frustration, rejection and violence, in an echo of the Avenger's pathology. It suggests that somewhere beneath Joe's ordinary exterior there lurks something repressed that is 'just as the Avenger is'.

Although Hitchcock sometimes appeared to be telling interviewers what they wanted to hear, it is nevertheless clear that he was interested in psychoanalysis. At the same time, the representation of psychoanalysts themselves is not particularly positive. Hitchcock seems to have been healthily sceptical about the authority wielded by psychoanalytic professionals, which is of a piece with his previously discussed attitudes towards the legal profession. In *Spellbound*, Dr Murchison (Leo G. Carroll), the owner of the psychiatric clinic, turns out to be the villain, while in *Vertigo*, Scottie's (James Stewart) nervous breakdown and subsequent neurotic behaviour resist treatment and end in tragedy.

Although in *Spellbound*, *The Wrong Man*, *Psycho* and *Marnie* the insights of psychoanalysis are to a great extent validated, the analysts themselves are

For *Spellbound* (1945), which Hitchcock called a 'another manhunt wrapped up in pseudo-psychoanalysis', the artist Salvador Dali was commissioned to design dream imagery. © ABC Photography Archives.

often untrustworthy characters. *Spellbound* seems to echo populist misgivings about psychoanalysis by suggesting that the institutions in which psychoanalysis is practised breed unprincipled self-interest (Dr Murchison – Leo G. Carroll), lechery and life-denying cynicism (Dr Fleurot – John Emery), and over-intellectualism (Dr Petersen – Ingrid Bergman – nicknamed 'the human glacier' by Fleurot). While this view is undoubtedly reductive, it is also one way in which psychoanalysis is reproached by its latterday opponents, such as Frederick Crews (1995) and Jeffrey Masson (1984).

Likewise, parts of Jay Presson Allen's script for *Marnie* sound like protofeminist diatribes against psychoanalysis, yet psychoanalysis is shown to have solved the mystery of her disturbing dreams and also, apparently, her problems with her sex life. A lengthy scene takes place with Marnie (Tippi Hedren), a frigid kleptomaniac, sitting up in bed while would-be lover/analyst Mark Rutland (Sean Connery) tries to talk her around to accepting a psychoanalytic cure. Marnie has noticed his reading matter: *Frigidity in Women* and *The Psychopathic Delinquent*. 'Have you read them', asks Mark? 'I don't need to read that muck to know that women are stupid and feeble and that men are filthy pigs', Marnie retorts. She accuses Mark of having 'a pathological fix on a woman who's not only an admitted criminal but who screams if you come near her' and calls him 'sick'. 'What about your dreams, Daddy dear?', she asks. In the course of her speech Marnie reveals her own familiarity with psychoanalysis, which she claims comes not from reading books, but from watching movies. 'You'll have me up on my poor paralysed legs by the next scene', she chides Mark. However, by the end of this scene she is held tightly in his arms, sobbing 'Help me!', negating her earlier independence of mind.

When asked by Peter Bogdanovich about *Marnie*, Hitchcock laid emphasis on the possibilities of understanding and curing neurosis through psychoanalysis, rather than on the problematic nature of Rutland's authority over Marnie: 'I feel that eventually, when he'd gotten the background of the girl, the fetish would eventually die away and be taken over by a genuine relationship. The only ambiguity was how long it would take to cure her' (in Bogdanovich, 1997, p. 538). As with *The Wrong Man*, Hitchcock seems to have consciously approved a happy (if conservative) end to a story which suggests radical criticisms of the social structure. However, by the time of *Vertigo* (1957), the optimism with which both Hitchcock's films and American society viewed psychoanalytic treatment seems to have dissipated: neither listening to Mozart nor enduring therapy can bring about Scottie's readjustment to society (Freedman, 1999). Psychosis has, in keeping with Freud's later views on it, a tragic outcome involving a compulsion to repeat.

Much ingenuity has gone into psychoanalytic readings of Hitchcock's films. David Sterritt manages to link the 'O' at the end of *Psycho, Vertigo, Rear Window* (an 'O' sound) with both castration and anality by invoking psychoanalytic theory. Even Arbogast (Arb-O-gast in Sterritt's reading) and Beethoven's Eroica (Er-O-ica) symphony are taken as evidence of *Psycho*'s hidden Freudian symbolism. 'If there is any doubt', he writes, 'of Hitchcock's scatological turn of mind throughout Marion's ordeal, a close-up of her first car's number plate lays it to rest: it is ANL-709, the numbers cushion an anus-like zero between two more substantial digits' (Sterritt, 1993, p. 106). Given the dominance of psychoanalytic interpretations of Hitchcock's films, it seems pertinent to ask whether there are any limits on the ways in which the films can be said to bear out the insistent logic of Oedipus, the phallus, anality, the law of the father, castration, voyeurism, fetishism, scopophilia and the *objet petit à* (terms which make up the chief lexicon of psychoanalytic theory).

In the light of the above, a number of criticisms have been directed at so-called cine-psychoanalysis (which is inspired by the writings of Jacques Lacan, a latterday interpreter of Freud). Many of the criticisms of Lacanian film theory are discussed specifically in relation to interpretations of Hitchcock's films which have occupied a privileged role in debates about psychoanalysis and cinema for the last 30 years. First, it has been argued that the films are often used to illustrate a general theory and that their particularities easily get lost. Richard Maltby argues that '"Hitchcock" . . . becomes no more than an element in a Lacanian theoretical procedure' (Maltby, 1995, p. 437). The theory itself assumes the form of a master narrative, ironically given the postmodern suspicion towards such narratives professed by many of the theorists themselves. As Judith Mayne wonders:

> How many times does one need to be told that individual film x, or film genre y, articulates the law of the father, assigns the spectator a position of oedipal desire, marshals castration anxiety in the form of voyeurism and fetishism, before psychoanalysis begins to sound less like the exploration of the unconscious and more like a master plot?
>
> (Mayne, 1993, pp. 68–9)

Raymond Durgnat, commenting on *Psycho*, notes that there is a 'popular idea that the real meaning of Norman's knife is that it's a phallus'. He goes on to point out that 'this too quickly assumes that if a sexual analogy with a detail is *possible*, it *must* be in play, it must contribute *most* of its meaning and emotion and it *must* have determined its choice' (Durgnat, 2002, p. 112, original italics). Gilles Deleuze and Felix Guattari (1983) have also objected to the imposition of the Oedipal matrix on to all forms of modern narrative, arguing for a more radical interpretation of psychoanalysis. Many Lacanian scholars reproach cine-psychoanalysts with a faulty understanding of the theory itself. Joan Copjec (1995) and Slavoj Žižek (2001) have demonstrated that Lacan's concept of the gaze has been misrepresented in work by Laura Mulvey and many others in their discussions of Hitchcock's films. Lacan's theory (influenced by Schopenhauer and Hegel) does not unproblematically lend itself to the Marxist-feminist appropriation of it by Mulvey and others, although it does connect Hitchcock's work to wider currents of European romantic thought which are readily identifiable in the films (Mogg, 1999).

Just because psychoanalytic criticism claims to unmask a fetishistic (compulsive and illusory) relationship between films, spectators and the social world doesn't mean that such criticism is immune from becoming a fetish itself. Ironically, if psychoanalysis is right, criticism may very well take this form. It is then possible that the Hitchcock films discussed, and the political causes sponsored by contemporary psychoanalytic critics, may have been ill served by the over-use of what Christopher Williams has called 'the clumsy club of ideology' (1994, p. 276). Richard Allen shares these suspicions, stating that 'with sufficient ingenuity, all films become available for a [psychoanalytic] feminist reading . . . but what then does this really tell us about the meaning of the film itself and, in particular, its particular significance?' (Allen, 1999, p. 141).

In conclusion, it needs to be stressed that some understanding of Freudian theory is useful to understand much of Hitchcock's work and to shed light on his worldview. In order to appreciate the interest which psychoanalysis held for Hitchcock, his collaborators and his audience, it is necessary to take a serious and non-dismissive attitude towards it. First, however, it is clear that in films such as *Spellbound*, *Marnie* and *Vertigo*, doubts about the ethics of psychoanalysis are raised which could apply to the use of psychoanalysis as an interpretive strategy used by critics studying his films. Richard Allen suggests that 'a film theorist who is informed by the ethics rather than just the theory of psychoanalysis will listen to what a film or text might say to them, rather than impose their theory upon it' (Allen, 1999, p. 142). Secondly, the use of the theory itself needs to be guided by more respect for the integrity and complexity of the philosophy underlying it. Freud and Lacan's theories, according to Hitchcock scholars such as Ken Mogg (1999), can more profitably be read alongside Hitchcock's films by taking into account the ideas of other thinkers such as Schopenhauer and Bergson. Thirdly, as Hitchcock's films often suggest, psychoanalytic critics could do well to reflect on the idea that blindness can easily be mistaken for insight.

7 Audiences and identification

Psychoanalytic critics in particular are apt to write as though their nuanced and sophisticated interpretations have a normative claim on the spectator. However, as one aphorism has it, critics search for significance, the public look for pleasure and the industry want money from a film. Although the public is more cine-literate and more educated than before, it is still motivated chiefly by the promise of pleasure, often of a visceral kind. As Hitchcock understood, it is only in the wealthier metropolitan areas that intellectual opinion has much effect on box office. As he became more successful, this audience constituency became more important to him. However, much of the time he was preoccupied, perhaps to a unique extent, with the problem of how to make his films in such a way as to involve the everyday public in their very construction. As the French philosopher Gilles Deleuze put it:

> [I]n the history of cinema Hitchcock appears as one who no longer conceives of the constitution of a film as a function of two terms – the director and the film to be made – but as a function of three: the director, the film and the public which must come into the film, or whose reactions must form an integrating part of the film.
>
> (Deleuze, 1986, pp. 62–3)

Hitchcock's interviews are full of references to his audience, many of which are not very flattering. However, his view of audiences is that their tastes are changing and becoming more sophisticated. So while Hitchcock was often near the cutting edge of mainstream film-making, sometimes to the extent that he felt pulled back by the demands of his audiences, he nevertheless acknowledged that audience responses are not immutable but are subject to evolution. He often referred to his expectation that the audience would respond emotionally rather than intellectually to his films, but even then, he did not see this emotional response as isolated from historical development. This is illustrated in an exchange between Hitchcock and Charles Samuels:

> Samuels: 'Your style seems to me to require some sophistication in anyone who wishes to appreciate you work.'
> Hitchcock: 'Yes. I don't expect the average spectator to go beyond his emotional reaction . . . this may explain why occasionally one of my films is indifferently received and then a year later, it becomes a classic.'
> (Samuels, 1972, p. 234)

Similarly, in a *Sight and Sound* article from 1937 called 'On Directing', he emphasises the idea of audience response as an evolutionary process when he writes, 'Popular taste . . . does move; today you can put over scenes that would have been ruled out a few years ago. . . . You can get comedy out of your stars, and you used not to be allowed to do anything which might knock the glamour off them.' Nevertheless, he complains, 'I must say that in recent years I have come to make much less use of obvious camera devices. I have become more commercially minded; afraid that anything at all too subtle may be missed. I have learnt from experience how easily small touches are overlooked' (in Gottlieb, 1997, p. 257). He concludes the article by saying that 'I hope in time to have more freedom still – if audiences will give it to me' (ibid., pp. 261–2).

On more than one occasion Hitchcock had suggested that his audience were not capable of appreciating his talents. *Murder!* (1930), for instance, with its innovative use of subjective sound and imaging, 'was an interesting film and was quite successful in London. But it was too sophisticated for the provinces' (in Truffaut, 1965/1986, p. 97). Ian Cameron and Victor Perkins once commented to him, 'You expect quite a lot of your audience.' Hitchcock replied, 'For those who want it. I don't think films should be looked at *once*' (in Cameron and Perkins, 1963, p. 5). When interviewed by the magazine *Cinema* in 1963, which the interviewer assured him was for 'the intelligent picture-goer', Hitchcock sarcastically asked, 'are there intelligent picture-goers?' (in Gottlieb, 1997, p. 285). Merely being popular did not satisfy Hitchcock's film-making ambitions. In a 1938 article for *The Listener*, he had expressed his view that 'the power of universal appeal has been the most retarding force of the motion picture as an art. In the efforts of the maker to appeal to everyone, they have had to come down to the common simple story with the happy ending.' Hitchcock felt that this formula was not conducive to the types of film he would ideally like to make as he went on to point out that, 'the moment they begin to become imaginative, then they are segregating their audience' (ibid., pp. 190–1).

He argued that there could be no great progress in mainstream film-making until there had been changes in the cinema audience, saying: 'motion pictures would be a source of much richer enjoyment, as is the case in the other arts, if the audience were aware of what is and what is not well done' (ibid., p. 217). As already noted, he also advocated the teaching of film in schools to foster the appreciation of film art. He asserted that there would be 'no radical change until there is a change in audiences. This can only come from the classroom; it's a job for the educators, not the moviemakers' (in Bouzereau, 1993, p. 164).

Hitchcock was fascinated by the idea of studying and analysing his audiences. He conceived detailed demographic analyses of the audience years before the Hollywood studios would take up the idea. Already, by 1935 he was dreaming of 'a corps of investigators who would discover and report on the trend and fluctuation of taste and audience reaction in the key centres of the country and of the world. . . . Through these I would have my fingers on the public pulse, find out what was wanted, and make my plans accordingly' (in Gottlieb, 1997, p. 175). In addition to the articles and interviews which regularly appeared in more specialist film publications, such as *Film Weekly*, Hitchcock talked to the general public about his influences and techniques in newspapers and magazines with a broad general readership. These included *Good Housekeeping*, *London Evening News*, *London News Chronicle*, *The Daily Express*, *Evening Standard*, *Cosmopolitan* and *Harper's Bazaar*. The articles he wrote and the interviews he gave transcended showbiz trivia and attempted to raise the level of public understanding about cinema.

As we have seen in Chapter 4 when speaking of 'contracts', Hitchcock was very aware of his different relationships to his audience: the tradesman/craftsman, selling his wares and tending to the public image of his product; the director who informs and educates his audience about the nature of his art; and the moralist, teaching his audience a lesson about the dangers of complacency. This last aspect of the director's relationship with his audience raises an interesting question: do Hitchcock's films address their audiences in a critical tone? Films which contained social criticism were more highly regarded by influential critics such as John Grierson in Britain and Bosley Crowther in America, who felt that cinema should be concerned with moral issues. O.B. Hardison, in an article called 'The Rhetoric of Hitchcock's Thrillers', argues that the art elements of Hitchcock's films are concerned with 'learning' and 'insight' – aspects which challenge and make demands on the audience. Hitchcock's attempts to please his audience and to go with the grain of their expectations is downgraded to mere 'rhetoric' (Hardison, 1967, p. 138). Similarly, Wood writes that:

Some of Hitchcock's finest work is flawed by compromises that, in an
artist free of 'commercial' constraints, would appear neurotic, the result
of a reluctance to allow certain disturbing implications to be fully explored,
but which Hitchcock encourages us (sometimes, in interviews, explicitly) to
regard as the result of external pressures, fears of alienating his audience . . .

(Wood, 1989, p. 219)

Wood praises the films for their capacity to arouse 'disturbing emotions'
and trade in 'subversive implications' but damns them for their failure of
nerve in not taking these elements further (ibid.).

Many of the critics who reviewed Hitchcock's films for the more
upmarket publications judged film-makers on their willingness to risk
upsetting their audiences by questioning their beliefs and attitudes. As
already noted, Hitchcock felt that critical approval was an element of
box-office success and from time to time he and his writers appeared to
be raising questions about the values required to be a good citizen in
society, an aspect of his work which was duly noticed by the reviewers and
later praised by critics such as Sarris and Wood (Kapsis, 1992). In contrast
to the portrayals of mob mentality in *The Lodger* (1926), where an innocent
man is hounded almost to death by an angry crowd, films such as *The Man
Who Knew Too Much* (1934), *Rear Window* (1954) and *The Birds* (1963)
emphasise a central character's development from complacent carefree
existence to one which is socially aware and responsible. His anti-Nazi
films, such as *Foreign Correspondent* (1940) and *Saboteur* (1942), exemplified the narrative structure to be found in many of his films such as *The 39
Steps* (1935), *The Lady Vanishes* (1938) and *Notorious* (1946), of ordinary
people leading ordinary lives confronted with a political threat to their
country and becoming actively involved in a struggle against fascism. He
wrote in *Stage* magazine that he aimed to give the public 'good, healthy,
mental shake-ups'. This, he said, is because, 'civilisation has become so
screening and sheltering that we cannot experience sufficient thrills at first
hand. Therefore to prevent ourselves becoming sluggish and jellified, we
have to experience them artificially, and the screen is the best medium for
this' (in Gottlieb, 1997, p. 249).

Taking up this theme, Andrew Sarris (1968) discusses Hitchcock as a
critic of bourgeois complacency. The implication of *The Birds*, for instance,
is that the balance between nature and humankind may be suddenly and
violently upset. The complacent Melanie Daniels (Tippi Hedren) needs to
be 'taught a lesson'. In the trailer for the film, Hitchcock humorously
discusses the ways in which man has exploited or mistreated birds, while
professing a hypocritical love of them. The trailer neatly combines
Hitchcock's moralist persona with his entrepreneurial one, as it makes a

subtle and ironic criticism of his society's attitude to nature as well as selling the idea of a new Hitchcock picture. He delivers his speech, which he describes as preparation for 'a lecture' on the subject, in a book-lined study with a caged bird prominently on view:

> *Originally, there were many varieties of birds on earth. Some have become extinct. The great hawk . . . the famous Dodo bird, have all disappeared. Actually, they didn't exactly disappear – they were simply killed off. But of course this is nature's way – man himself simply hastens the process along wherever he can be of help. . . . But man has not been unmindful of his debt to the birds. We have honoured our feathered friends in many ways. We cage birds and show them off proudly in most of our zoos. The turkey is traditionally our guest of honour at Thanksgiving.*

He then saunters over to a dinner table and proceeds to tuck into a roast chicken. But as he eats, his expression changes and he goes on to say, 'I have begun to feel very close to the birds and I have developed real sympathy for our little . . .', and here his speech falters. He continues: 'I have come to realise how they feel when . . .' At this point the jaunty background music begins to jar and Hitchcock walks over to the caged bird and continues to preach about how much man has done for the birds. As he points at the bird in the cage, it bites his finger and the soundtrack begins to introduce some of the electronic squawks used in the film to generate fear in the audience. 'Now why would he do that?', exclaims Hitchcock. The squawk-ing on the soundtrack becomes louder and suddenly there is a cut to Tippi Hedren as Melanie bursting into the room, slamming the door shut with a look of terror on her face, crying 'they're coming, they're coming'.

For the remainder of the trailer, Hitchcock's civilised persona, discours-ing with mock-pomposity on the birds is replaced by dark images of circling birds from the opening credits of the film accompanied by the electronic squawking. Titles appear over these images asking, 'What is the SHOCKING mystery of the birds? They massed in their thousands and tens of thousands. WHY? What was their evil intent? SUSPENSE AND SHOCK BEYOND ANYTHING YOU HAVE EVER SEEN OR IMAGINED!' Through the trailer, Hitchcock and his publicity department posed a series of enigmas for the audience which, it assumes, will be resolved in the course of the story itself (in fact they are never answered in the film). The trailer finishes by mentioning Hitchcock's name twice in connection with the film which is billed as 'Alfred Hitchcock's *The Birds*' and followed by some text in quotation marks which reads: '*The Birds* could be the most terri-fying motion picture I have ever made.' The quotation is signed, 'Alfred Hitchcock'. The linking of Hitchcock's name to the film is important; it is part of the sales pitch for the film and reinforces his reputation for mystery, suspense and shock. The quote at the end of the trailer carries a promise of satisfaction from the Master in person.

In the end the film was deemed a failure on account of poor box-office performance and the audience responded negatively to the film's ambiguous ending which showed the car-bound protagonists starting their journey with the sunrise clouded by a mass of screeching and fluttering birds. The fact that the 'shocking mystery of the birds' 'massed in their thousands and tens of thousands' was never accounted for in the story marked a breakdown in the contract Hitchcock had built up with his followers. He received letters of bitter disappointment, and even requests for refunds from his loyal audience who regularly attended the latest Hitchcock film. He had established a reputation for reliability among his followers and this was now in jeopardy. Hitchcock's artistry was even compared to Stravinsky and Dizzy Gillespie by one fan who went on to complain that Hitchcock had 'violated one of [his] fundamental rules' by failing to explain why the birds attacked (Kapsis, 1992, pp. 66–7). Evidently, Hitchcock, who had coached his audience well in the rules of his game, was not permitted to rewrite them.

By the 1960s, the mass audience was drifting away from the cinema and Hitchcock's decision to make a more experimental film was partly influenced by his perception that he would have to review his approach. Audience research suggested that among the most regular cinema-goers were a small, well-educated and socially elite group of college students whose tastes did not necessarily coincide with those of the majority. Art house films were growing in popularity with French films such as *Wages of Fear* (1954) and *God Created Woman* (1956) taking respectable box office. The film-makers and studios still aimed to attract much larger audiences into the cinema and from time to time succeeded. However, throughout the 1960s they went less frequently than the small but loyal clique of cinephiles who attended regularly and who read the critics avidly (Ray, 1985).

Hitchcock's bid to capture the intellectual high ground, if necessary at the cost of alienating his more mainstream audience, was not altogether a misplaced ambition. If he was to survive in a decade which saw most of his generation, including such box-office stalwarts as Howard Hawks and John Ford, out of touch with the new audience, he would have to try to adapt to the sudden shift of the regular audience into a smaller, more exclusive niche market. Shortly before making *The Birds* Hitchcock had arranged to view a number of films by notable European art film-makers. These included Bergman's *The Virgin Spring* (1959), Antonioni's *L'Avventura* (1960) and Godard's *A Bout de Soufle* (1959) (Kapsis, 1992). Against the urging of his screenwriter, Evan Hunter, he insisted on an ending for *The Birds* which would be 'poetic' and 'meaningful'. The ambiguity and gloomy atmosphere of the film's ending may have alienated many of Hitchcock's regular audience but it was perfectly in tune with the ideals of the newly fashionable European art film (Kapsis, 1992, pp. 76–9).

Hitchcock arranged for *The Birds* to première in the United States at the Museum of Modern Art, and in Europe at the Cannes film festival – a firm indication of the level of his artistic ambitions in making the film as well as revealing his strategy to re-brand himself for the 1960s, a decade characterised by its generation gap between 'squares' and hip youth counter-culture. Although the film was not well received commercially or critically in America on its release, his attempts at a European-style art film have been judged much more favourably in the intervening years. Yet, the question remains concerning Hitchcock's orientation to the general audience at the time.

Did Hitchcock mean to teach his audiences a lesson? His own assertion that *The Birds* was a warning against complacency, would suggest this, although on this occasion his audience did not pay much attention to it. Furthermore, his professed critical stance was not found convincing by many intellectuals. Wood saw the film as Hitchcock's 'most "serious"' but complained that 'the development which the film appears to offer – the stripping away of the layer of complacent superficiality – never really materialises' (Wood, 1989, p. 222). There are other films, however, in which it is also possible to see some didactic intent. A counterpart to the critique of complacency in *The Birds* is found in such films as *The Man Who Knew Too Much*, *The 39 Steps* and *Foreign Correspondent*, which indicate the importance of social responsibility and anti-fascism. These are stories about individuals who go energetically, but complacently, about their lives. The turning point comes when, through an event beyond their control, they are torn from their comfortable surroundings and undertake an adventure. In the course of their journey they are politicised and develop some notion of social citizenship. This is when they arrive at some mature understanding of their relationship to others and to the world. Hitchcock's commitments to social responsibility and to political awareness stemmed partly from his aforementioned involvement with the Film Society in the 1920s which aimed to promote these values. Of Hitchcock's British films, *The Man Who Knew Too Much*, which was produced by the chief ideologist of the Film Society, Ivor Montagu, is perhaps the clearest statement of these ideals.

The first version of *The Man Who Knew Too Much* is Hitchcock's most didactic early film, and promotes the ideas of social responsibility and political awareness without appearing to propagandize. Its underlying dynamic is the development undergone by the Lawrence family (Leslie Banks and Edna Best) and their friend Clive (Hugh Wakefield), following the kidnap of their daughter, Betty (Nova Pilbeam). Thinking only of themselves at the start of the narrative, the Lawrences refuse to help the police with their investigation into an assassination plot being hatched by the kidnappers, as they fear it might harm their daughter. Through witnessing the cruelty and sadism of the kidnappers while held captive, Bob and Clive come to feel a moral duty to stop the assassination. Jill's scream during the concert at the Albert Hall where the assassination is due to take place is her final realisation that the crime has moral implications for her so terrible that she cannot help but respond to it by crying out in public to put the gunman off his aim, regardless of the danger to her daughter.

Hitchcock's films are also notable for their inclusion of an audience within a scene in his films, particularly in sequences set in theatres or cinemas. He cuts away from the action on stage, to an audience of spectators, including them in the spectacle. However, what is interesting about the representation of the audience in the frame is that spectatorship and participation often threaten to collapse in on one another. The scream from the audience in the climactic concert hall sequence of *The Man Who Knew Too Much* (1934 and 1956), is one example. The charged and eventually fatal interaction between performer and audience as Mr Memory (Wylie Watson) in *The 39 Steps* takes questions and finally a bullet from the audience at an East End music hall is a reminder that Hitchcock spent his childhood at theatrical events where audience participation was normal, expected and sometimes riotous.

In a number of the films, art and life become interwoven as the barrier between spectacle and spectatorship is breached. For example, in *Saboteur*, an armed villain is chased into a cinema where he attempts to get away by running across the screen. Hitchcock shows the tiny silhouette of the saboteur in the corner of the movie screen, holding a gun. In the next instant a gun is fired onscreen just as the saboteur shoots into the audience, killing a man who slumps on to his wife's lap. She momentarily assumes that he, like the rest of the audience, is convulsed with laughter at the film. However, when she realises that he has been shot, she lets out a loud scream which sets off a panic in the cinema. The film, meanwhile, continues to echo the real-life situation, 'Get out before I shoot you', the cuckolded husband yells onscreen as members of the audience start to flee the cinema.

Rear Window is also built around the main character's movement from a curious but amoral spectatorship to his morally committed participation in the events which unfold in front of him. The plot involves an invalid, Jeff (James Stewart), staring out of his apartment window and into the windows of the block opposite. He is a photographer by trade and he begins to observe the goings on opposite him through a telephoto lens, eventually getting caught up in a thriller scenario. The film exemplifies Hitchcock's technical skill at psychologically 'manipulating' his audience. On more than one occasion, notably in his interview with Truffaut concerning *Rear Window*, Hitchcock pointed out the importance of the lessons he had learned from the celebrated Kuleshov experiment, which was used to teach the principles of montage to Russian film students in the 1920s. Hitchcock's anecdote about the film here sheds some light on his working methods in general: 'You have an immobilised man looking out', he tells Truffaut, 'that's one part of the film. The second part shows what he sees and the third part shows how he reacts.' He then goes on to compare this scenario with the famous 'Kuleshov experiment' described by the Russian film-maker Pudovkin: 'You see a close-up of the Russian actor Ivan Mosjukine. This is immediately followed by a shot of a dead baby. Back to Mosjukine, he looks hungry. Yet, in both cases, they used the same shot of the actor; his face was exactly the same.' Hitchcock then compares this to a scene in *Rear Window* where he shows a close-up of James Stewart looking at a dog being lowered into a basket, then cutting back to Stewart, 'who has a kindly smile. But if in the place of the little dog you show a half-naked girl, exercising in front of her open window, and you go back to smiling Stewart again, this time he's a dirty old man!' (in Truffaut, 1965/1986, p. 321).

Rear Window raises questions about the ethical relationship of the audience to the institution of popular cinema itself. Jeffries, like the average cinema audience, desires to be the spectator at the scene of murder, romance and sex. Like the cinema audience, he is not disappointed. Unlike the cinema audience, his voyeuristic fascination leads him from secure spectatorship to life-threatening participation, as the murderer from the 'screen' opposite, crosses the line over into his domain as a member of the 'audience' and tries to kill him. In the course of the film, Jeff will wonder 'if its ethical to watch a man with binoculars and a long focus lens', and Lisa will reply that she's not much on 'rear window ethics' but she considers them 'a couple of ghouls' who are disappointed because a woman has not apparently been killed and sliced up.

This reading is supported by reference to the design of the film set containing one apartment block where the spectating is done (the audience) and another apartment block opposite (the cinema screen), where the sex, violence and romance takes place. It can also be supported by numerous lines of dialogue in the film, such as his nurse Stella's (Thelma Ritter) line: 'We've become a race of peeping toms, what people oughta do is get outside their own house and look in for a change.' Furthermore, the use of point of view in the film would also bear out this reading as the bulk of the camera shots are from Jeffries' apartment block on to the other side and not vice versa.

Rear Window provides a particularly graphic instance of a tendency present in many of Hitchcock's films which is to involve the audience as participants in a moral theorem. The involvement of the audience is facilitated greatly by the patterns of cutting which encourage intense identification with a particular character through repeated close-ups of his or her face, followed by point of view shots, indicating what they can see. For *Psycho* (1960), Hitchcock insisted on the use of a 50 mm lens because it was the nearest equivalent to the field of vision of a human being. Marshall Schlom, the script supervisor, claimed that this was because 'he wanted the camera being the audience all the time, to see as if with their own eyes' (Mogg, 1999, p. 158). Furthermore, Marion, Sam, Norman and Lila are presented to the audience as humanly imperfect characters, 'people whom we can like and admire and identify with and criticise – and in whose hopes, experiences and errors we recognise our own and those of our friends and acquaintances, and through which we can easily start reviewing our moral codes, our culture, our "ideology"' (Durgnat, 2002, p. 31).

It has been argued in this book that Hitchcock was very much aware of the importance of the audience for his films. This has been evident from his skilful command of public relations and the way in which his films seem to forge contracts with the audience. However, we have seen in this chapter that Hitchcock's films involved some subtle understandings and negotiations of the art of spectatorship. As we will see in the next chapter, the nuances of spectating are sustained even in what is popularly thought to be Hitchcock's most blatant and graphically horrifying film, *Psycho*, of which Hitchcock claimed 'I was directing the viewers. You might say I was playing them, like an organ' (in Truffaut, 1965/1986, p. 417). Yet how much control was he really able to exert over the production and reception of his films? This question, among others, can usefully be addressed by taking a closer look at *Psycho*.

8 Hitchcock's legacy: *Psycho* and after

Hitchcock's public fame today rests to a great extent on the enduring appeal of one film in particular, *Psycho* (1960). *Psycho* is also one of the most analysed of all films. Countless interpretations of it have appeared in print. Among the most notable close readings of the film itself are Durgnat (1974; 2002), Rothman (1982) and Wood (1989). In this chapter, however, the aim is to place the film within a wider context, taking into account its production and reception histories. A consideration of the film's production history will show the extent to which Hitchcock relied on the contributions of others. It will also highlight the importance of industrial constraints and imperatives. Bill Krohn (2000) has criticised the notion that the director merely sat back as his team shot the film precisely as he had planned it. Instead, Hitchcock relied to a considerable extent on contributions from others and was frequently driven to deviate from his plans for practical reasons or as a result of pressure from studio executives.

In addition to the insights to be gained from a study of the film's production, the circumstances of the film's reception demonstrate that, once in the public domain, critics and audiences appropriated *Psycho* in a number of ways, many of them inconsistent with Hitchcock's intentions or expectations. A close look at the production and reception of the film enables us to put debates about Hitchcock's authorship and ownership of the meanings attached to his films on to a firmer footing. Stephen Rebello's (1990) book on *Psycho* gives a wealth of detail about the making of the film and draws out some of the everyday practical issues faced by Hitchcock. In order to complete the project he had first to negotiate relationships with business executives, collaborators and critics. He also needed to negotiate the social mores of his time and to stay abreast of changing fashions in the all-important new youth audience.

Although the film was an immediate success, earning over $9.5 million on its first US release, and is now Hitchcock's best-known film, it had a troubled production history. Paramount decided that the material was too

Janet Leigh as Marion Crane in *Psycho* (1960). Courtesy of Universal Studios Licensing LLLP.

downmarket and unsavoury for Hitchcock's more mainstream audience and tried to stop him from making the film. He was told that all the sound stages were booked and Paramount only allowed him to make the film when he agreed to self-finance the project. Executives at Paramount who had seen the film prior to its release pronounced his low budget thriller a failure and advised Hitchcock on a damage limitation strategy for booking the film into US cinemas. The hysteria that eventually accompanied the first screenings took Hitchcock by surprise, even though he had worked hard to promote the film. However, before long the film drew record profits, while Norman Bates achieved the status of a popular culture icon. Today it is even possible to buy *Psycho* shower curtains and other Bates motel paraphernalia for home decoration.

Hitchcock's decision to make *Psycho* was taken against a backdrop of crisis in the American film industry. Competition with television and other leisure activities, combined with mass migration to suburbs (where there were, as yet, few cinemas) had brought about a disastrous slump in cinema attendance figures. In 1929, cinema admissions had reached 95 million a week but this had decreased to below 20 million a week in the 1960s and 1970s. Hitchcock's move into television in 1955 with *Alfred Hitchcock Presents* proved to be an effective survival strategy for him. The television show had been the brainchild of his agent Lew Wasserman and would guarantee Hitchcock's fame and success during the period of Hollywood's decline. Durgnat (2002) suggests that the black humour in his TV shows appealed to an emerging youth counter-culture, perhaps partly as a reaction against some of the more earnest socially conscious drama of the 1950s such as *The Men* (1950), *Marty* (1956) and *The Defiant Ones* (1958).

Psycho capitalised on Hitchcock's television production methods and began as an extended version of the *Alfred Hitchcock Presents* pioneering formula. In the TV shows, Hitchcock would take a sinister short story with a startling twist at its conclusion, and adapt it quickly and cheaply. Each episode was prefaced by a humorous appearance from the director. This aspect of the formula was adapted for the *Psycho* marketing campaign in the droll trailer where Hitchcock shows the audience around the Bates Motel. He acts like a lugubrious estate agent, tantalising his audience with suggestions of the horror that took place, but holding back until the final moment when shrieking violins sound and an image of a screaming face fills the screen.

The film cost only $800,000 to make and was an example of Hitchcock's famed parsimony. He saved money wherever he could and bought the rights to Robert Bloch's novel anonymously for $9,500 which maximised his profit on the deal. He shot the film very quickly, often using two cameras for the scenes, an approach he adapted from TV filming. The film also had great narrative economy in the way he pared down the opening scenes during the cutting process by eliminating many sequences from the original shooting script. However, a few of the elements of the film were worthy of a major film budget: seven full days were budgeted for the shooting of the shower scene, Saul Bass's credits were expensive and Hitchcock paid Herrmann a $17,500 fee.

Hitchcock had been inspired to make a horror film by the success of companies like American International Pictures and Hammer Film Productions, which made big profits on low-budget horror films which catered to the changing tastes of the audience. As Stephen Rebello puts it, 'such shockfests as *Macabre* (1957), *I Bury the Living* (1957) and *The Curse of Frankenstein* (1957) drew crowds while many Hollywood "A"-budget pictures barely drew flies' (Rebello, 1990, p. 22). *Psycho* was Hitchcock's first exploration into the horror genre, although its success was so considerable that during the pre-release of *The Birds* (1963) he was acclaimed as a long-standing master of the genre. The film was based on a novel by Robert Bloch. Hitchcock made few changes to the book, which contained many of the elements which critics attributed to Hitchcock's genius. As Rebello explains, Bloch 'had sexed up and Freudianised the Gothic, revitalising such creaky elements as the rattletrap Old Dark House, the stormy night, and the crackpot madwomen locked in the dank basement' (1990, p. 12). Hitchcock used an inexperienced writer, Joseph Stefano, to work on the script. Although Hitchcock coached Stefano in screenwriting, many of the most celebrated ideas and shots in the film arose out of dialogue between the two men on a weekly, sometimes daily, basis. According to Raymond Durgnat, Stefano was selected 'not just to write down what Hitchcock dictated, but for his rare skill at dialogue rich in "colour" (implications about character and background), at which Hitchcock felt himself not gifted' (Durgnat, 2002, p. 28). Stefano suggested one of the main changes to the book, the idea of beginning the story with Marion Crane (Janet Leigh) rather than Norman Bates (Anthony Perkins) and that the film should open with a helicopter shot over the city of Phoenix, Arizona. This was then combined with Hitchcock's idea of the camera going in through the hotel room window. Stefano also claims that he had pointed out to Hitchcock the importance of the overhead shot of the Arbogast (Martin Balsam) murder. This now famous scene also had input from the designer Saul Bass before Hitchcock himself decided on the precise details of shooting it. Hitchcock also acknowledged Bloch's contributions (at least against those of Stefano), for he later told writer Charles Higham that '*Psycho* all came from Robert Bloch. Joseph Stefano contributed dialogue mostly, no ideas' (in Rebello, 1990, p. 40).

Hitchcock's inspiration for *Psycho* also included Henri-Georges Clouzot's film *Les Diaboliques* (1954) which was the work of a gifted Hitchcock acolyte. One critic wrote that 'If director Henri-Georges Clouzot isn't the master of the suspense thriller today, then who is. True, Hitchcock is suaver; but this Frenchman is joltier, a master of timing and building an almost unbearable suspense' (ibid., p. 21). After critics claimed that Clouzot was stealing the master's thunder, Hitchcock started to take ideas from Clouzot.

He took the marketing concept from the film – 'Don't spoil the ending for your friends by telling them what you've just seen' and combined this with the idea of shooting in black and white and having a terrifying scene set in a bathroom (ibid.). The bathroom setting also provided Hitchcock with an opportunity to court controversy over the inclusion of a shot of a flushing toilet. This proved to be a major victory for Hitchcock over the censor and was seen by Stefano as a key effect in the unsettling of the American audience who had been brought up to think of even the sight of a toilet as disgusting. He said of the scene, 'This is where you're really going to find out what the human race is all about. We're going to start by showing you the toilet and it's only going to get worse' (ibid., p. 47).

The famous shower murder has subsequently been the subject of a major argument over its authorship, with Saul Bass claiming much of the credit for the scene. Immediately after the murder the camera shows blood being washed down the drain which dissolves to a shot of Marion's open, lifeless eye. The spiral effect of the water superimposed over the eye (which also 'rhymes' visually with the toilet flushing shot) has helped to fuel

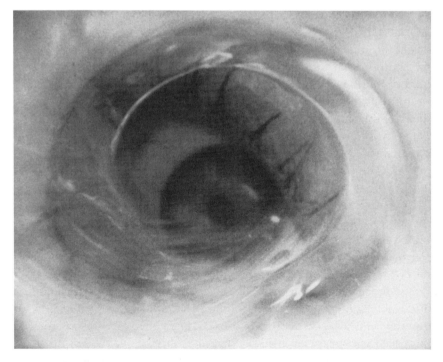

This dissolve from Janet Leigh's eye to the water washing her blood down a drain has been part of a controversy over the authorship of the whole shower scene in *Psycho* (1960). Courtesy of Universal Studios Licensing LLLP.

controversy over the authorship of the shower scene as it recalls the eye/ spiral motif created by Saul Bass for *Vertigo*'s (1957) credit sequence. In Stefano's script, the audience do not glimpse the attacker until after the murder. The script also provides the idea that the knife is never seen touching the body but instead 'offers a series of images and metaphors which make the sequence an attack on the spectator's vision, on the screen where the scene is being projected, and on the film itself' (Krohn, 2000, p. 225). In the scene's evolution, Hitchcock's next move was to invite Saul Bass to storyboard the scene as Stefano had written it. Bass introduced the image of the attacker as a silhouette and sketched in 'one high angle shot of the struggle with the curtain rod cutting across it, representing the boundary which the attacker has transgressed; the vertical lines of the water, and various low angle compositions built around head-on shots of the shower nozzle spewing down at the camera' (ibid.). However, in spite of the closeness of his storyboard to the finished scene, the claim later attributed to Bass in *The Sunday Times*, that he had directed the scene, is not accurate. Bass was not actually on set during the filming of the scene and the storyboard was not only the result of consultation with Hitchcock, it was also subtly changed in places during the actual filming. Where the storyboard had included a picture of Marion being stabbed in the back, Hitchcock had filmed this as an out-of-focus shot whereby Marion's body blocks the knife thrust. Where Bass sketched in the celebrated dissolve from the shower drain to Marion's eye, Hitchcock added a camera movement in the opposite direction to the bloody water going down the drain. Krohn concludes from his investigations that, 'despite the complexity of the shooting process and the important contributions of Stefano, Bass, Tomasini and cameraman John Russell, there is a singleness of intent that carries through from Stefano's first draft to the finished sequence' (ibid., p. 230). The evidence suggests that each of the collaborators contributed to the realisation of Hitchcock's overarching vision.

The contributions of Bloch, Rebello and Bass are thus integral to the success of this most 'Hitchcockian' film. However, perhaps the most important collaborative element in *Psycho* is the score by Bernard Herrmann which has achieved iconic status in its own right. Herrmann's music was startlingly original for a Hollywood film. He had taken the bold step of scoring the film for a string section only and later commented that this was in order to complement 'the black and white photography of the film with a black and white sound' (in Rebello, 1990, p. 187). The fast-paced opening music, with its rhythmic, driving quality, sets up an air of dread and near panic, even before the story has started. Hitchcock and Herrmann agreed to bring in the music used in the opening credits 'which tells the audience, who don't know something terrible is going to happen to the girl, that it's got to' (Herrmann, in Smith, 1991, p. 239). This is the key to Hitchcock's suspense strategy in the first part of the film: he allows Herrmann's music to suggest subtly and indefinitely that something frightening is going to happen to the heroine without disclosing exactly what it is.

Bernard Herrmann remarked that without the tense, edgy music as Marion drives through the rain to the Bates Motel, 'she could have been driving to the supermarket' (ibid.). Instead, the audience has the impression of a descent into hell as the strings pound away, relentlessly increasing the sense of dread. Hitchcock's notes to his sound crew gave very detailed instructions about how the sound was to be manipulated to get the maximum effect from the audience:

> When we reach the night sequence, exaggerate passing car noises when headlights show in her eyes. Make sure that the passing car noises are fairly loud, so that we get the contrast of silence when she is found by the roadside in the morning. . . . Just before the rain starts there should be a rumble of thunder, not too violent, but enough to herald the coming rain. Once the rain starts, there should be a progression of falling rain sound and a slow range of the sound of passing trucks. . . . Naturally, wind shield wipers should be heard all through from the moment she turns them on. . . . The rain sounds must be very strong, so that when the rain stops, we should be strongly aware of the silence and odd dripping noises that follow.
>
> (in Rebello, 1990, p. 137)

Hitchcock understood the importance of Herrmann's music to the film, remarking that '33% of *Psycho* is due to the effect of the music' (in Smith, 1991, p. 241).

Having completed his film with no support from Paramount, Hitchcock then had to deal with the studio executives' negative reaction to the film's initial screening. According to Stephen Rebello, the screening 'did not shake their view that the film was a decidedly minor, forgettable, even disreputable Hitchcock effort' (Rebello, 1990, p. 148). However, having invested so much of his own money in the film, Hitchcock geared himself up for his most extensive marketing campaign yet. Rebello notes that 'Hitchcock maximised his three most exploitable commodities: the title, the shock climax, and his own persona as a roly-poly ringmaster of a macabre circus of horrors' (ibid., p. 149). He insisted, following Clouzot's example, that no members of the audience were to be allowed in after the start of the film, and enforced this by a contract which had to be signed by cinema managers. The negative critical response to the film on its release has been attributed to Hitchcock's insistence on treating members of the press and the public alike. In a marked change of attitude from his earlier efforts to woo the press, he denied them previews and refused them entry if they arrived late. This resulted in a spate of negative reviews. Dwight Macdonald in *Esquire*, for instance, described the film as 'a reflection of a most unpleasant mind, a mean, sly, sadistic little mind' (ibid., p. 165).

Once the critics had recovered from their rough treatment, the consensus began to shift in *Psycho*'s favour with Andrew Sarris in *The Village Voice* describing it as 'the first American movie since *Touch of Evil* (1958) to stand in the same creative rank as the great European films'. In addition to its powerful demonstration of Hitchcock's formal technique, Sarris also saw the shower murder as a moral statement. He later saw it as Hitchcock's most effective warning against complacency: 'When murder is committed in a gleamingly sanitary motel bathroom during a cleansing shower, the incursion of evil into our well laundered existence becomes intolerable. We may laugh nervously or snort disgustedly, but we shall never be quite so complacent again' (Sarris, 1968, pp. 57–8). His interpretation was reinforced by reports from all over the country that people had become afraid to enter their showers after seeing the film. One woman wrote angrily to Hitchcock that after seeing *Psycho* her daughter had refused to shower. Hitchcock's response was 'get her dry cleaned then'.

Although Hitchcock was not the first to insist the audience be admitted only at the start of a feature film, his campaign to make latecomers wait was very influential for the film industry in America. Before *Psycho*, audiences could roll in when it suited them (this was considered particularly convenient for people who did shift work). One or two films, such as *Gone With the Wind* (1939), *Hamlet* (1948) and *The Bad Seed* (1956) had used strict admissions policies, and, in the case of *The Bad Seed*, had made a plea for the audience not to spoil the ending by telling their friends about it. However, Hitchcock's film was unusual in that it applied this audience discipline to a low-budget horror film as if it were a much more dignified cultural artefact. In the process, Hitchcock can take a measure of the credit for having transformed audience viewing habits (see Hawkins, 2002).

Hitchcock's showmanship reached a new zenith with a promotional film, made specially for cinema owners, called *The Care and Handling of Psycho*, which carried detailed instructions on how (and how not) to exhibit the film. Many cinemas played tapes of Hitchcock speaking to the audience as they queued outside and as they went in they passed a lifesize cut-out of the director holding a sign saying 'Please don't spoil the ending – it's the only one we have'. Linda Williams (1994) has argued that the long wait many had experienced while queuing for the film contributed to the suspense experienced while watching it. One of the most famous stories concerning the film's release concerned an incident at Woods Theatre in Chicago where a torrential downpour caused a near riot in the queue for the film which was only averted when Hitchcock happened to hear of the situation and requested that free umbrellas be distributed to everyone waiting, thereby generating extensive press coverage the following day for the stunt.

During public screenings, members of the audience frequently became hysterical. They fainted, stormed out, and ran up and down the aisles. Truffaut suggested that the relative lack of spoken dialogue paid dividends in foreign markets where distracting dubbing or subtitles had to be used. He argued that '*Psycho* is particularly universal because it's a half-silent movie; there are at least two reels with no dialogue at all' (Truffaut, 1965/ 1986, p. 436). This point seems borne out by the film's record box office all over the world, generating an additional $6 million in foreign rentals on its release. Hitchcock's verdict on his film reinforced his earlier insistence on the importance of film form over content:

> *People will say, 'It was a terrible film to make. The subject was horrible,*
> *the people were small, there were no characters in it.' I know all of this,* ·
> *but I also know that the construction of the story and the way in which it*
> *was told caused audiences all over the world to react and become emotional.*
> *(in Truffaut, 1965/1986, p. 434)*

Whatever Hitchcock owed to Henri-Georges Clouzot, Robert Bloch, Joseph Stefano, Saul Bass, Bernard Herrmann or any of the team who worked on it, *Psycho* remains a testimony to his demonic skills as an engineer of human unease and terror.

Psycho spawned three disappointing sequels, *Psycho II* (1983), *Psycho III* (1986) and *Psycho IV* (1990). More interesting and successful was the work of the artist Douglas Gordon who in 1993 produced an art gallery installation called *24 Hour Psycho*. The work consisted of a huge screen, on to which *Psycho* was projected. However, Gordon had slowed the film down so that it took a whole day for the film to run its length. The installation was a striking success with critics and the gallery-going public as it traded simultaneously on the familiarity of the images combined with a very freakish and distancing new experience of them. Stripped of their proper narrative rhythm, the images stun the viewer with the beauty of their composition which now appears in the form of a moving sculpture.

Gus Van Sandt's *Psycho* (1998), a postmodern pastiche of the original, was heavily backed by its producers, Universal Studios. However, it failed to make much of an impression on the younger audience at which it was aimed in spite of the use of contemporary language, stars and colour photography. The updated *Psycho*, referred to as an 'anti-remake' by Van Sandt, faithfully reproduces much of the original film. As Naremore observes, it copies 'most of the original film's script, decoupage, music, and design, sometimes duplicating the tiniest details of mise-en-scène (such as the word 'okay' printed at the top of a newspaper sticking out of Marion Crane's pocket)'. Yet Naremore, like most critics and members of the audience, was unimpressed, describing the film as 'academic and not at all scary' (Naremore, 2002, p. 389).

'How could a director, especially one not devoid of talent, make a virtually shot-by-shot copy of *Psycho* that is so uninteresting?' asked William Rothman (1999, p. 30). It's an interesting question – if the film is so close a copy of the original, how could it fail to elicit the same response as the original? At least part of the answer lies in the areas where Van Sandt has made changes. Parts of the remake are simply more upfront than the original. Where Hitchcock had observed that the use of black and white film made the bloodshed more bearable for the audience, Van Sandt's film revels in the gory possibilities of showing blood on colour film. Where Norman was only shown spying at Marion in the original, in the remake he is masturbating. Instead of the mysterious and shocking, but unidentified, book which Marion finds in Norman's room in the 1960 version, the update has a pornographic magazine. There are also changes in the photography. As Naremore explains, 'the Panavision framing and colour photography create a kind of "noise" or extra layer of information that somewhat obscures the bold graphic conflicts and relatively abstract geometric quality of Hitchcock's work'. Furthermore, Van Sandt interpolates images of his own into some of the most important montage sequences – storm clouds in the shower scene, a woman in a g-string and a cow in the middle of a road when Arbogast is stabbed (Naremore, 2002, p. 393). All of these changes violate a fundamental principle in Hitchcock's film-making which is to make the audience imagine things that they don't actually see by feeding their imagination with just the right amount of information.

Perhaps the most damaging creative decision made by Van Sandt was to cast Vince Vaughn as Norman Bates. Vaughn copies the gestures of Anthony Perkins but has an altogether different body type and demeanour. As Naremore quips, 'when Sam and Norman battle in the cellar, Norman looks like a full back wearing a fright wig' (ibid., p. 391). Naremore also points out that a very subtle doubling which works at three different levels in the original is also destroyed. At various times, Perkins as Norman resembles Marion (when he looks feminine), Sam (when he looks handsome) and Mother's skeleton (when he looks thin and angular). All of this is possible because Perkins himself was a very complex, and inwardly conflicted, bisexual actor with a range that seems beyond that of Vaughn. Aware of the film's status as a cult classic in gay sub-culture (see, for instance, Doty, 2000), Van Sandt, a high-profile gay director, decided with actress Julianne Moore that the character of Lila, Marion's sister, should be a lesbian (Bolton, 2002, p. 1). However, this does not really come across in the film and rather than further the stereotype of Norman as a gay, mother-obsessed psychopath, Van Sandt seems to have gone out of his way to indicate the former's heterosexuality by including the masturbation scene.

Appropriations of *Psycho* seem inevitable and justified since the film never really 'belonged' to Hitchcock during its production and it certainly didn't all come from his imagination. The film contained a complex reworking of traditional melodramatic themes and gothic motifs, contributed by Bloch and Stefano and augmented by modernist visuals from Bass and a modernist-influenced score from Herrmann. Once on release, Hitchcock attempted to influence its reception through marketing and PR as it became appropriated by a variety of audiences (mainstream public, gay sub-culture, reviewers, academics, film directors and artists) for their own ends. *Psycho* generates new meanings as it comes into contact with new audiences and changed cultural contexts. Its significance evolves as the film exists in a state of becoming. Hence it is not only Hitchcock's death which prevents the achievements of *Psycho* being repeated. It is also the decline of the Hollywood studio system and the hot house, repressive atmosphere of 1950s society which enabled the perverse pleasures of the film to ripen.

Nevertheless, Hitchcock himself remains the necessary, if not sufficient, element in the success of his films. Brian De Palma has claimed that 'dealing with Hitchcock is like dealing with Bach – he wrote every tune that was ever done. Hitchcock thought up practically every cinematic idea that has been used and probably will be used in this form' (Rebello, 1990, p. 192). If this is so, then it becomes clear that Hitchcock's films will retain a privileged place in film culture. They show little sign of diminished appeal for a new generation who have come into contact with them largely through television, video, the Internet and DVD. The media may have moved on but the meanings and visceral shocks generated by Hitchcock's films continue to inspire and excite, as well as to make considerable profits as their creator so fervently wished. Today the adjective Hitchcockian denotes not simply a type of film, but also a worldview and a cultural sensibility which has perhaps come to dominate the modern world. Detached, ironic, blackly humorous, stylish and self-aware, the sensibility manifested in *Psycho* is aligned to modern metropolitan existence at the start of the twenty-first century. Hitchcock has transcended his status as a film-maker to become a cultural phenomenon of the first order.

Hitchcock's reputation as a popular entertainer is unassailable. Yet, because of the deeper social, political and aesthetic currents in his work, he has also taken up a position at the forefront of the most challenging avant-garde art and intellectual life. Exhibitions such as *Notorious: Alfred Hitchcock and Contemporary Art* (MOMA Oxford, 1999) and *Fatal Coincidences* (Montreal Museum of Fine Arts, 2000) confirm that his films have been enthusiastically embraced by new generations of experimental artists as one of their own. At the start of a new millennium, Hitchcock's films straddle the divide between solid mainstream entertainment and some of the most difficult, challenging and esoteric forms of contemporary culture. The films constitute a cultural institution, reassuring and dependable, yet at the same time as unsettling and disturbing as ever.

© ABC Photography Archives.

Bibliography

Allen, Richard (1999) 'Psychoanalytic Film Theory' in T. Miller and R. Stam (eds), *A Companion to Film Theory* (Oxford: Blackwell).

Allen, Richard (2000) 'The Lodger and Hitchcock's Aesthetic', *Hitchcock Annual*, 2001/2, pp. 36–78.

Astruc, Andre (1948/1968) 'The Birth of a New Avant Garde: Le Camera Stylo' in Peter Graham (ed.), *The New Wave* (London: Secker and Warburg/BFI).

Barr, Charles (1993) *Ealing Studios*, revised edition (London: Studio Vista).

Barr, Charles (1999) *English Hitchcock* (Moffat: Cameron and Hollis).

Barthes, Roland (1977) *Image, Music, Text*, trans. Stephen Heath (London: Fontana).

Bazin, André (1968) 'The Evolution of Film Language' in Peter Graham (ed.), *The New Wave* (London: Secker and Warburg).

Bazin, André (1972) 'Hitchcock Against Hitchcock' in Albert J. LaValley (ed.), *Focus on Hitchcock* (Englewood Cliffs, NJ: Prentice-Hall).

Belloc Lowndes, Marie (1996) *The Lodger*, ed. Laura Marcus (Oxford: Oxford Paperbacks).

Bellour, Raymond (2000) *The Analysis of Film*, ed. Constance Penley (Bloomington and Indianapolis: Indiana University Press).

Bergfelder, Tim (1996) 'The Production Designer and the *Gesamtkunstwerk*: German Film Technicians in the British film Industry of the 1930s' in Andrew Higson (ed.), *Dissolving Views: Key Writings on British Cinema* (London: Cassell).

Bogdanovich, Peter (1997) *Who the Devil Made It* (New York: Alfred A. Knopf).

Bolton, Chris (2002) 'Psycho 98' at www.24framespersecond.com/reactions/ films p/psycho98.html

Booth, Michael (1964) *Hiss the Villain: Six English and American Melodramas* (London: Eyre and Spottiswoode).

Bouzereau, Laurent (1993) *The Alfred Hitchcock Quote Book* (New York: Citadel Press).

Cameron, Ian and V.F. Perkins (1963) 'Interview with Hitchcock', *Movie*, 6 4–6.

Christopher, Nicholas (1997) *Somewhere in the Night: Film Noir and the American City* (New York: The Free Press).

Cobley, Paul (2002) *Narrative* (London: Routledge).

Cogeval, Guy (2001) 'Welcome to the Museum Mr Hitchcock', in Dominique Païni and Guy Cogeval, *Hitchcock and Art: Fatal Coincidences* (Montreal: Montreal Museum of Fine Arts).

Cohen, Paula Marantz (1995) *The Legacy of Victorianism* (Lexington, KY: University of Kentucky Press).

Copjec, Joan (1995) *Read My Desire: Lacan Against the Historicists* (Cambridge, MA: MIT Press).

Corber, Robert (1993) *In the Name of National Security: Hitchcock, Homophobia and the Political Construction of Gender in Postwar America* (London and Durham, NC: Duke University Press).

Crews, Frederick (1995) *The Freud Wars: Freud's Legacy in Dispute* (London: Granta).

Deleuze, Gilles (1986) *Cinema 1: The Movement Image*, trans. B. Habberjam and H. Tomlinson (London: Athlone Press).

Deleuze, Gilles and Felix Guattari (1983) *Anti-Oedipus: Capitalism and Schizophrenia* (Minneapolis: University of Minnesota Press).

De Rosa, Steven (2001a) 'Getting It Right about *The Wrong Man*' at http://members.aol.com/vistavision/wrongman.html

De Rosa, Steven (2001b) 'Hitchcock's Italian Connection' at http://members.aol.com/vistavision/italianconnection.html

Deutelbaum, Marshall (1986) 'Finding the Right Man in *The Wrong Man*' in Marshall Deutelbaum and Leland Poague (eds), *A Hitchcock Reader* (Ames, IA: State University Press).

Domarchi, Jean and Jean Douchet (1959) 'Entretien Avec Alfred Hitchcock', *Cahiers du Cinéma*, **XVII** (102) December 17–29.

Doty, Alexander (2000) *Flaming Classics: Queering the Film Canon* (London: Routledge).

Durgnat, Raymond (1974) *The Strange Case of Alfred Hitchcock or The Plain Man's Hitchcock* (London: Faber and Faber).

Durgnat, Raymond (2002) *A Close Look at Psycho* (London: BFI).

Eisner, Lotte (1969) *The Haunted Screen* (London: Thames and Hudson).

Ettedgui, Peter (1999) *Production Design and Art Direction* (London: Rotovision).

Freedman, Jonathan (1999) 'From *Spellbound* to *Vertigo*: Alfred Hitchcock and Therapeutic Culture in America' in J. Freedman and R. Millington (eds), *Hitchcock's America* (Oxford: Oxford University Press).

Freud, Sigmund (1979) 'A Child is Being Beaten' in *Penguin Freud Library. Vol. 10: On Psychopathology* (Harmondsworth: Penguin).

Freud, Sigmund (1985) 'The Uncanny' in *Penguin Freud Library. Vol. 14: Art and Literature* (Harmondsworth: Penguin).

Freud, Sigmund (1991) 'Civilisation and Its Discontents' in *Penguin Freud Library. Vol. 12: Civilisation, Society and Religion*, trans. James Strachey (Harmondsworth: Penguin).

Freud, Sigmund (2002) *The Psychopathology of Everyday Life,* trans. Anthea Bell (Harmondsworth: Penguin).

Gans, Herbert J (1999) *Popular Culture and High Culture: An Analysis and Evaluation of Taste* (New York: Basic Books).
Gamman, Lorraine and Merja Makinen (1992) *Female Fetishism* (London: Lawrence and Wishart).
Garrett, Greg (1999) 'Hitchcock's Women on Hitchcock: A Panel Discussion with Janet Leigh, Tippi Hedren, Karen Black, Suzanne Pleshette and Eva Marie Saint', *Literature/Film Quarterly,* **27** (2) 79–89.
Gibbs, John (2002) *Mise-en-Scène: Film Syle and Interpretation* (London: Wallflower Press).
Goldman, William (1996) *Adventures in the Screen Trade: A Personal View of Hollywood* (London: Abacus).
Gottlieb, Sidney (ed.) (1997) *Hitchcock on Hitchcock: Selected Writings and Interviews* (Los Angeles: University of California Press).
Gottlieb, Sidney (2000) 'Early Hitchcock: The German Influence', *Hitchcock, Annual,* 1999/2000, pp. 100–130.
Gunning, Tom (1986) 'The Cinema of Attraction: Early Film, Its Spectator and the Avant Garde', *Wide Angle,* **8** (3–4) 63–70.

Hallam, Julia and Margaret Marshment (2000) *Realism and Popular Cinema* (Manchester: Manchester University Press).
Hardison, O.B. (1967) 'The Rhetoric of Hitchcock's Thrillers' in W.R. Robertson (ed.), *Man and the Movies* (Baton Rouge, LA: Louisiana State University Press).
Haskell, Molly (1973) *From Reverence to Rape* (New York: Holt, Reinhart and Winston).
Hawkins, Joan (2002) ' "See It From the Beginning": Hitchcock's Reconstruction of Film History' in Sidney Gottlieb and Christopher Brookhouse (eds), *Framing Hitchcock* (Detroit, MI: Wayne State University Press).
Highsmith, Patricia (1950/1999) *Strangers on a Train* (London: Vintage).
Hirsch, Foster (1981) *Film Noir: The Dark Side of the Screen* (New York: Da Capo).
Hitchcock, Alfred (1936) 'Why I make melodramas' at http://www.labyrinth. net.ac/~muffin/melodramas_c.html
Hunter, Evan (1997) *Me and Hitch* (London: Faber and Faber).

Jancovich, Mark (1996) *Rational Fears: American Horror in the 1950s* (Manchester: Manchester University Press).
Jensen, Paul M. (2000) *Hitchcock Becomes Hitchcock: The British Years* (Baltimore, MD: Midnight Marquee Press Inc).

Kapsis, Robert A. (1992) *Hitchcock: The Making of a Reputation* (Chicago: University of Chicago Press).
Krohn, Bill (2000) *Hitchcock at Work* (London: Phaidon).

LaValley, Albert J. (1972) *Focus on Alfred Hitchcock* (Englewood Cliffs, NJ: Prentice-Hall).

Lebeau, Vicky (2001) *Psychoanalysis and Cinema: The Play of Shadows* (London: Wallflower Press).

Leff, Leonard J. (1987) *Hitchcock and Selznick* (New York: Weidenfield & Nicolson).

McCann, Graham (1996) *Cary Grant: A Class Apart* (London: Fourth Estate).

McGilligan, Patrick (1997) *Backstory 3: Interviews with Screenwriters* (Los Angeles: University of California Press).

McLaughlin, James (1986) 'All in the Family: Alfred Hitchcock's Shadow of a Doubt' in Marshall Deutelbaum and Leland Poague (eds), *A Hitchcock Reader* (Ames, IA: Iowa State University Press).

Maltby, Richard (1995) *Hollywood Cinema* (Oxford: Blackwell).

Masson, Jeffrey (1984) *The Assault on Truth* (New York: Pocket Books).

Mayne, Judith (1993) *Cinema and Spectatorship* (London: Routledge).

Modleski, Tania (1988) *The Women Who Knew Too Much* (London: Routledge).

Mogg, Ken (1999) *The Alfred Hitchcock Story* (London: Titan Books).

Montagu, Ivor (1972) 'Interview with Peter Wollen, Sam Rohdie and Alan Lovell', *Screen*, **13** (2) 71–113.

Mulvey, Laura (1975) 'Visual Pleasure and Narrative Cinema', *Screen*, **16** (Autumn) 6–18.

Napper, Lawrence (2000) 'British Cinema and the Middlebrow' in Ashby and Andrew Higson (eds), *British Cinema: Past and Present* (London: Routledge).

Naremore, James (ed.) (1993) *North by Northwest* (New Brunswick, NJ: Rutgers University Press).

Naremore, James (2002) 'Remaking Psycho' in Sidney Gottlieb and Christopher Brookhouse (eds), *Framing Hitchcock* (Detroit, MI: Wayne State University Press).

Païni, Dominique and Guy Cogeval (2001) *Hitchcock and Art: Fatal Coincidences* (Montreal: Montreal Museum of Fine Arts).

Prawer, S.S. (1980) *Caligari's Children: The Film as Tale of Terror* (Oxford: Oxford University Press).

Price, Theodore (1992) *Hitchcock and Homosexuality: His 50-Year Obsession with Jack the Ripper and the Superbitch Prostitute – a Psychoanalytic View* (Metuchen, NJ: Scarecrow Press).

Prince, Stephen (2001) *Movies and Meaning*, second edition (Boston: Allyn and Bacon).

Ray, Robert (1985) *A Certain Tendency of the Hollywood Cinema 1930–1980* (Princeton, NJ: Princeton University Press).

Rebello, Stephen (1990) *Alfred Hitchcock and the Making of Psycho* (New York: Dembner Books).

Renov, Michael (1980) 'From Identification to Ideology: The Male System of Hitchcock's *Notorious*', *Wide Angle*, **4** (1) 32.

Rohmer, Eric and Claude Chabrol (1992) *Hitchcock: The First Forty-Four Films* (Oxford: Roundhouse Publishing).

Rothman, William (1982) *Hitchcock: The Murderous Gaze* (Cambridge, MA: Harvard University Press).

Rothman, William (1999) 'Some Thoughts on Hitchcock's Authorship' in *Alfred Hitchcock: Centenary Essays* (London: BFI).

Russell, Mark and James Young (2000) *Film Music: Screencraft* (London: Rotovision).

Ryall, Tom (1996) *Alfred Hitchcock and the British Cinema* (London: Athlone Press).

Samuels, Charles (1972) *Encountering Directors* (New York: Charles G.P. Putnam's Sons).

Samuels, Robert (1998) *Hitchcock's Bi-Textuality: Lacan, Feminisms and Queer Theory* (Albany, NY: State University of New York Press).

Sarris, Andrew (1968) *The American Cinema* (New York: Dutton).

Scorsese, Martin (1999) in *Sight and Sound*, special supplement on Hitchcock, July.

Silver, Alain and Elizabeth Ward (1980) *Film Noir: An Encyclopaedic Reference Guide* (London: Bloomsbury).

Sloan, Jane (1995) *Alfred Hitchcock: The Definitive Filmography* (Berkeley, CA: University of California Press).

Smith, Steven C. (1991) *A Heart at Fire's Centre: The Life and Music of Bernard Herrmann* (Los Angeles: University of California Press).

Spoto, Donald (1976) *The Art of Alfred Hitchcock* (New York: Hopkinson and Blake).

Spoto, Donald (1983) *The Dark Side of Genius: The Life of Alfred Hitchcock* (London: Frederick Muller).

Sterritt, David (1993) *The Films of Alfred Hitchcock* (Cambridge: Cambridge University Press).

Sweet, Matthew (1999) 'Introduction' to *The Woman in White* by Wilkie Collins (Harmondsworth: Penguin).

Taylor, John Russell (1978) *Hitch: The Life and Works of Alfred Hitchcock* (London: Faber and Faber).

Thomson, David (1979) 'The Big Hitch: Is the Director a Prisoner of His Own Virtuosity?', *Film Comment*, **15** (2) March–April 26–9.

Truffaut, François (1965/1986) *Hitchcock by Truffaut* (London: Paladin).

Waldman, Diane (1983) ' "At last I can tell it to someone": Feminine Point of View and Subjectivity in the Gothic Romance Film of the 1940s', *Cinema Journal*, **23** (2) Winter 29–41.

Warhol, Andy (1976) *From A to B and Back Again: The Philosophy of Andy Warhol* (London: Pan Books).

Weis, Elizabeth (1985) 'The Evolution of Hitchcock's Aural Style and Sound in *The Birds*' in Elizabeth Weis and John Belton, *Film Sound: Theory and Practice* (New York: Columbia University Press).

Wexman, Virginia Wright (1986) 'The Critic as Consumer: Film Study in the University, *Vertigo* and the Film Canon', *Film Quarterly* **39** (3) Spring 32–41.

Williams, Christopher (1994) 'After the Classic, The Classical and Ideology: The Differences of Realism', *Screen*, **35** (3) Autumn 275–92.

Williams, Linda (1994) 'Learning to Scream' in *Sight and Sound*, 4 (12) 14–17.

Wollen, Peter (1997) 'Compulsion', *Sight and Sound*, April.

Wollen, Peter (1998) *Signs and Meaning in the Cinema*, expanded edition (London: BFI).

Wood, Robin (1965) *Hitchcock's Films* (London: Zwemmer).

Wood, Robin (1989) *Hitchcock's Films Revisited* (London: Faber and Faber).

Yacowar, Maurice (1986) 'Hitchcock's Imagery and Art' in Marshall Deutelbaum and Leland Poague (eds), *A Hitchcock Reader* (Ames, IA: Iowa State University Press).

Žižek, Slavoj (ed.) (1992) *Everything You Always Wanted to Know about Lacan but Were Afraid to Ask Hitchcock* (London: Verso).

Žižek, Slavoj (2001) *The Fright of Real Tears* (London: BFI).

Zola, Emile (1868/1962) *Thérèse Raquin*, trans. Leonard Tancock (Harmondsworth: Penguin).

Further reading

Allen, Richard and Sam Ishii-Gonzales (2004) *Hitchcock: Past and Future* (London: Routledge).

Barr, Charles (1996) 'Hitchcock's British Films Revisited' in Andrew Higson (ed.), *Dissolving Views* (London: Cassell).

Brill, Lesley (1988) *The Hitchcock Romance: Love and Irony in Hitchcock's Films* (Princeton, NJ: Princeton University Press).

Cohen, Paula Marantz (1995) *Alfred Hitchcock: The Legacy of Victorianism* (Lexington: University of Kentucky).

Fawell, John (2001) *Hitchcock's Rear Window: The Well-Made Film* (Illinois: Southern Illinois Press).

Gottlieb, Sidney and Christopher Brookhouse (2002) *Framing Hitchcock* (Detroit, MI: Wayne State University Press).

Hitchcock O'Connell, Pat and Laurent Bouzereau (2003) *Alma Hitchcock: The Woman Behind the Man* (New York: Berkeley Books).

McArthur, Colin (2000) 'The Critics Who Knew Too Little: Hitchcock and the Absent Class Paradigm', *Film Studies*, **2** (Spring).

McGilligan, Patrick (2003) *Alfred Hitchcock: A Life in Darkness and Light* (West Sussex: John Wiley).

Smith, Susan (2000) *Hitchcock: Suspense, Humour and Tone* (London: BFI).

Index